Notes on English Literature

Chief Adviser: JOHN D. JUMP
Professor of English Literature in the University of Manchester
General Editor: W. H. MASON
Lately Senior English Master, Manchester Grammar School

THE POETRY OF GERARD MANLEY HOPKINS

H. C. SHERWOOD

*Senior Staff Tutor, Extra-Mural Department,
Manchester University*

BASIL BLACKWELL
OXFORD

Printed in Great Britain by
WESTERN PRINTING SERVICES LTD, BRISTOL
and bound by
KEMP HALL BINDERY, OXFORD

CONTENTS

GENERAL NOTE

This series of introductions to the great classics of English literature is designed primarily for the school, college, and university student, although it is hoped that they will be found helpful by a much larger audience. Three aims have been kept in mind:

(A) To give the reader the relevant information necessary for his fuller understanding of the work.

(B) To indicate the main areas of critical interest, to suggest suitable critical approaches, and to point out possible critical difficulties.

(C) To do this in as simple and lucid a manner as possible, avoiding technical jargon and giving a full explanation of any critical terms employed.

Each introduction contains questions on the text and suggestions for further reading. It should be emphasized that in no sense is any introduction to be considered as a substitute for the reader's own study, understanding, and appreciation of the work.

INTRODUCTION

I

In approaching the poetry of Gerard Hopkins it is important to stress how Victorian a poet he is. The fact that his poetry, edited by his friend Robert Bridges, was not published in a collected edition until 1918 and was not widely read until the 'thirties, should not be allowed to obscure how firmly Hopkins's work is rooted in his age. His contemporaries, Tennyson, Browning, Meredith, Whitman, Patmore, Matthew Arnold were remarkable for their boldness in the handling of verse. The virtuosity of Browning and Whitman in their so different ways attracted no small section of the contemporary reading public. What the reactions of that public to the work of Hopkins would have been it is impossible to say, but the formation of Browning societies to tease out the obscurities of Browning's poetry (and he could be quite as difficult as Hopkins to elucidate) gives us some assurance that poetry making severe demands in adjustment both to widely differing tempers and to technical innovation was not lacking in readers. It is not possible in a short space to establish Hopkins firmly in his period. A few pointers, however, may be useful. Of these it will be convenient to discuss first those social preoccupations that are present in the poetry but not dominant.

Hopkins's love of England pervades his poetry but the narrower patriotism, in its turn related to his admiration for soldierly qualities, links him with the jingoist vein in the popular verse of his time:

Not the pleasure, the pay, the plunder,
But country and flag, that flag I am under—
There is the shilling that finds me willing
To follow a banner and fight for honour.

(No. 156)[1]

This is not from an early poem; it was written in 1885, the period of the 'terrible' sonnets. The opening of the sonnet *The Soldier*, 'Yes, Why do we áll, seeing of a soldier, bless him? bless / Our redcoats, our tars?' is only matched in our century by Mr. Day Lewis's 'Yes, why do we all, seeing a communist, feel small?' Associated with such verse is the more obtrusive admiration elsewhere in his work for masculine strength and physical beauty.

On a more disturbing level, and here Hopkins is at one with his great contemporaries, is his concern with the ugliness and suffering born of industrialisation. As a young priest he served at various times in Liverpool, Glasgow, Leigh and Manchester. The son of cultivated parents he had led a sheltered early life both at home and at Oxford. It is known that he preferred to be moved from parish duties in Oxford to work in the north of England. The shock that he received when he was confronted by the slums of the North was extreme, the measure of it may be taken from his letters to Bridges and from the late sonnet *Tom's Garland*. It is worth noting that the warmth of his feeling for the people of Leigh in Lancashire where he spent three months in 1879 made his stay there a happier one than in any of the parishes in which he served: 'The place is very gloomy but our people hearty and devoted.'

After his experience of the industrial north it is true to

---

[1] All quotations from the poems are taken from the fourth edition of *The Poems*, ed. W. H. Gardner and N. H. Mackenzie, O.U.P., 1967.

say that his poetry only occasionally expresses the untroubled delight in the natural world that he had achieved
in his earlier poetry. Not that the darkening of his poetry
is to be attributed mainly to this cause, but it is an important contributing factor as the following comment in
a letter to R. W. Dixon shows:

> My Liverpool and Glasgow experience laid upon my
> mind a conviction, a truly crushing conviction, of
> the misery of town life to the poor and more than to
> the poor, of the misery of the poor in general, of the
> degradation even of our race, of the hollowness of this
> century's civilization: it made even life a burden to me
> to have daily thrust upon me the things I saw.

Hopkins's hostility to liberalism and to Gladstone himself is evident in many passages in the letters. He restrained
himself with difficulty in writing of Gladstone. He felt
'gloomy' in 1880 when Gladstone was asked to form his
second ministry. Again in 1885 he wrote 'Do not let us
talk politics, it kills me, especially under the present
Prime Minister.' In reply to a letter of Bridges suggesting
that Gladstone ought to be beheaded on Tower Hill and
buried in Westminster Abbey he writes 'Ought he now to
be buried in Westminster Abbey? As I am accustomed
to speak too strongly of him I will not further commit
myself in writing'. He makes a private reservation in his
notebooks not to speak intemperately against Gladstone.
It is a misconception to see Hopkins as a figure isolated
from social and political facts. He was a contemplative,
a religious, but also a man troubled and anxious about the
way things were drifting in English society.

There is ample evidence to show the strain that he felt in
Ireland where anti-English feeling naturally ran high, e.g.,

> I wear-
> y of idle a being but by where wars are rife.

He finds himself reluctantly on Gladstone's side over Home Rule:

> Matthew Arnold has a fine paper in the Nineteenth [*i.e. the Nineteenth Century*] on the Home Rule Bill, a temperate but strong condemnation of the G[rand] O[ld] M[an]. It might with truth be much stronger. Not but what I wish Home Rule to be: it is a blow at England and may be followed by more, but it is better that should be by peaceful and honourable means with at least the possibility of a successful working which otherwise may come by rebellion, bloodshed, and dishonour. . .
>
> (Letter to his friend Baillie).

Here as always Hopkins calls a spade a spade, shows firm judgment and prescience.

Of Hopkins's conversion something must be said. His decision in 1866 to leave the Church of England to go over to Rome was, of course, the decision that determined the subsequent pattern of his life. Here, too, it is necessary to see the decision in its context. The high thinking, the conscience searching, that we find in Hopkins are characteristic of the circles in which he moved. To try to live out the ideal of a gentleman, fastidious, responsible, self-disciplined, seems to have been the rule rather than the exception among the more serious Oxford students.

What we know of Hopkins at home and at school suggests that the grain of his character was such as to make Oxford a congenial home for him. The spiritual crisis that he experienced as an undergraduate has to be set against an Oxford torn by religious controversy. Hopkins's parents 'were High Church of the moderate school' and Gerard from his arrival at Balliol in 1862 until the middle of 1865 remained of their persuasion. According to his friend, Addis, it was in the early summer of 1865 that they discovered that their 'faith in Anglicanism had really gone'. A little over a year later Hopkins was received into the Catholic Church; so was Addis in the same year. Crises of faith were characteristic of Hopkins's friends, and while they led to a variety of solutions, the tensions were clearly of a similar order. Hopkins in exploring the evidence for his beliefs and in making the most difficult of choices was not by any means alone and has to be seen in the perspective of a whole pattern of excited religious controversy that had continued, unabated, from the early days of the Oxford or Tractarian movement of the early 1830's.

Neither as a priest in training, nor as an ordained priest was he cut off from the life of his times. He was only too painfully aware of the more sombre side of Victorian England, was perturbed by political tendencies, and, of course, acutely sensitive to the moral and theological speculations of his contemporaries. His letters are particularly satisfying in the range of their responsiveness to what is going on about him.

It is important to stress the many-sidedness of Hopkins's interests because it is tempting in considering his poetry to treat him as a special case, as a lonely and eccentric figure, whereas the very manner of his letters, the alertness of mind, the critical balance, the penetration of passing comments on events that made him the valued correspondent of Bridges, should be sufficient warning against taking him in this way. A sense of the brutal defacement of the English landscape, of the deformation of the image of Man by industrialization, the vision of a paradisal freshness still available, the delight in the mighty world of eye and ear are not constricting material for a poet to handle and are as relevant now as when he was writing.

2

Turn now to Hopkins's artistic leanings. He came of a family in which the practice of the arts was encouraged. Hopkins himself was pulled by the visual arts; his pencil drawings are of an exquisite quality. It is characteristic that on moral grounds he turned away from what might have been his vocation. His interest in music was life-long. His admiration for Purcell that finds expression in his sonnet-tribute to Purcell's memory, points to a certain temperamental affinity. In later life he attempted composition and submitted his work to the inspection of Sir Robert Stewart, an eminent musician of the day. Hopkins was endowed with an all-round richness of sensibility that nourishes and pervades his poetry.

His responsiveness to the visual arts and the qualities of his own sketches provide a direct link with the kind of poetry he wrote. Hopkins has been described by Humphrey House as the most successfully pre-Raphaelite of the pre-Raphaelite poets. He was an admirer of Ruskin and like Ruskin developed considerable refinement in recording natural and architectural detail. He was also attracted by the work of the painter Millais. When opportunity allowed he visited exhibitions of work by contemporary artists and was free with his comments on them. As far as I am able to judge his perceptions were honest and acute, but the scope of his comments was relatively narrow and they are such as might be made by a follower of Ruskin.

It is not primarily the medievalism of the pre-Raphael-ite painters and poets that brings Hopkins's poetry close to them but their original insistence on the rejection of the renaissance and post-renaissance formalization of the natural world and the human form in favour of the inno-cent vision of the Italian primitives; their insistence on seeing the natural world, not through the eyes of a tradi-tion, but in its freshness of colour and form. Hopkins's notebooks are full of verbal descriptions of cloud-formations, sometimes with accompanying sketches, the jottings of a poet-painter, with here and there a loving detail recorded of the inscape, characteristic line, of a bluebell flower or an ash-tree spray. It is not surprising that Keats should have been a powerful shaping influence on his earliest poetry. And it is to be remembered that in so far as the pre-Raphaelites found much of their inspira-tion in literary works, Keats may be considered along with Ruskin as standing behind the Movement.

Ruskin in his *Modern Painters* stresses not only the exactness of the observation of artists in this school but their capacity to see below the surface to the wonder of creation as expressed in its detailed manifestations:

> From young artists nothing ought to be tolerated but simple bona fide imitation of nature. . . . Their duty is neither to choose, nor compose, nor imagine, nor experimentalize; but to be humble and earnest in following the steps of nature, and tracing the finger of God.

It is significant that Newman, in so many ways a model for Hopkins in his way of life, should have expressed his attitude towards the natural world in very similar terms.

In his *Apologia pro Vita Sua* Newman quotes from a sermon he had given in 1834:

> What would be the thoughts of a man who, when examining a flower, or a herb, or a pebble, or a ray of light, which he treats as something so beneath him in the scale of existence, suddenly discovered that he was in the presence of some powerful being who was hidden behind the visible things he was inspecting, who, though concealing his wise hand, was giving them their beauty, grace, and perfection, as being God's instrument for the purpose, nay, whose robes and ornaments those objects were, which he was so eager to analyse?

Hopkins with his preoccupation with inscape and instress appears to be striving for an even sharper definition than the pre-Raphaelites achieved of the kind of insights that intense contemplation of natural forms could yield. The point to be stressed is how very close Hopkins was, particularly in his attitude to the natural world, to a particular group of poets, artists and thinkers of his time.

3

Before we turn to an examination of individual poems it will prove useful to say something of Hopkins's interest in language and of his boldness in metrical experiment.

His earliest surviving poems, *The Escorial*, written when he was sixteen, and *A Vision of Mermaids* when he was eighteen, show a surprisingly assured command of the chosen traditional forms. Keats and Spenser are obviously the guiding influences.

He rang'd long corridors and cornic'd halls,
And damasqu'd arms and foliag'd carving piled.—
With painting gleamed the rich pilaster'd walls—.
Here play'd the virgin mother with her Child
In some broad palmy mead, and saintly smiled,
And held a cross of flowers, in purple bloom;
                                    (The Escorial, St. 10).

Even more astonishing is the range of vocabulary in *A Vision of the Mermaids*. It is peppered with the names of precious stones (beryl, garnet, 'sapphire molten-blue', 'dusk-deep lazuli', 'thick-pearlèd cords', 'turquoise-gemm'd', jacinthine, amethyst, 'pearly mist', crystalline, rubies, onyx), names of metals, and adjectives of colour with *rose* and *crimson* heading the list. The excess in itself, a kind of drugged exuberance, is promising and there are moments when one senses the future poet as in the lines—

Plum-purple was the west; but spikes of light
Spear'd open lustrous gashes, crimson-white.

He has a long way to go before he achieves the exquisite placing of 'the dappled-with-damson west' in the *Wreck of the Deutschland*, but one doesn't feel that *A Vision of the Mermaids* is merely an exercise. What these two early poems reveal is an excitement in the exploration and manipulation of language even though the effect is over-rich, over-emphatic.

Apart from the exploration of language that is natural to a poet of promise, Hopkins early showed a scholarly interest in the origins of words. Many of the first jottings in his surviving notebooks have to do with the roots of words. In his lifetime the study of etymology advanced steadily. He was sharply aware of this and kept in touch

with developments. One of his last letters was to Walter
Skeat, the great philologist. Hopkins's knowledge in this
field enabled him to release the potential of words. Much
of the pleasure in reading his poetry is to experience a
language that has been spring-cleaned. Layers of vague
and misty usage have been stripped off.

Hopkins became interested, too, in another developing
nineteenth-century field of study, that of dialect, and
along with it a concern for the purity of English, a movement in favour of the Anglo-Saxon element in the
language. Notice how skilfully Hopkins is able to make
dialect words like 'degged' or 'sillion' feel at home in his
poetry. They become part of the currency of his language
without affectation or any effect of the archaic. Hopkins
is the least literary of poets in his avoidance of allusive-
ness. 'The echos [*sic*]', he writes in criticizing Bridges, 'are
a disease of education, literature is full of them; but they
remain a disease, an evil'. His poetry is forthright and
this forthrightness is in part made possible by favouring
the Anglo-Saxon element in the language. It is characteristic of this poet, a brilliant classical scholar, that he should
favour what he regarded as the sinew of his native tongue.
He normally selects the *native* word as against one of
Latin origin, so that when a word from the Latin does
intrude it has a special force and justification.

The third and perhaps most important aspect of Hopkins's concern with language is his relating of the poet's
language to the spoken word. He rejects a language
reserved for poetry that is 'too full of untos, thereafters
and -eths' and is specially hard on the deliberately
archaic, 'We do not *speak* that way' (my italics). The
poet must forge his own language—beat it into the shape
he wants—but his language should be that of its age.

'The poetical language of an age should be the current language heightened, to any degree heightened and unlike itself, . . . but not an obsolete one.' However *heightened* the language of Hopkins is, the poems are as completely conceived in terms of the speaking voice as a violin sonata is for the violin. The freshness of Hopkins, his freedom from any kind of literary stuffiness, stems as much from the rhythmic originality and unexpectedness as from any other source: 'Take breath and read it with the ears, as I always wish to be read, and my verse becomes all right'. . . . 'My verse is less to be read than heard.' *Harry Ploughman* is 'altogether for recital, not for perusal', i.e. it requires alert and vigorous performance for its completion as a poetic experience.

It was the acuteness of Hopkins's ear for speech rhythms that encouraged him to evolve in 'sprung rhythm' a metrical system that suited his temperament. His concentration on the Anglo-Saxon element in English tended in itself to move him to draw on the stress-alliterative principle that governed English poetry until the fifteenth century. He put himself to learn Anglo-Saxon late in life after most of his finest poems had been written, but he had come across hints of a similar principle in nursery rhymes, in Shakespeare and Milton, and elsewhere in English poetry.

The foundation of sprung rhythm is simple. The attempt to systematise it by codification tends to lead to unnecessary difficulty. Once the basic notion is seized, close application, reading—aloud or with the ear—and alert persistence will sort out most problems of stress. In reading Hopkins's poetry what may seem eccentric on the page to the eye will usually prove acceptable to the ear when spoken, for example, when a word is broken between the ending of one line and the beginning of another, as with the word 'kingdom' in the first two lines of *The Windhover*. What sometimes looks clumsy on the page falls naturally into place when declaimed. In a famous letter to his friend R. W. Dixon Hopkins tells how his rector suggested that someone should write a poem on the wrecked Deutschland and then goes on to say:

> On this hint I set to work and, though my hand was out at first, produced one. I had long had haunting my ear the echo of a new rhythm which now I realised on paper. To speak shortly, it consists on scanning by accents or stresses alone, without any account of the number of syllables, so that a foot may be one strong syllable or it may be many light and one strong. I do not say the idea is altogether new; there are hints of it in music, in nursery rhymes and popular jingles, in the poets themselves, and, since then, I have seen it talked about as a thing possible in critics. Here are instances:

> > *Díng, dóng, béll;*
> >
> > Pússy's ín the wéll;
> >
> > *Whó pút her ín?*
> >
> > Líttle Jóhnny Thín.
> >
> > *Whó púlled her óut?*
> >
> > Líttle Jóhnny Stóut.

For if each line has three stresses or three feet it follows that some of the feet are of one syllable only. So too

> > *Óne, twó, Búckle my shóe,*

In Campbell you have

> Ánd their fléet alóng the *déep próudly* shóne
> It was tén of Ápril *mórn by* the chíme, etc.;

in Shakspeare

> Whý shd. *thís* désert bé?

corrected wrongly by the editors; in Moore a little melody I cannot quote, etc. But no one has professedly used it and made it the principle throughout, that I know of. Nevertheless to me it appears, I own, to be a better and more natural principle than the ordinary system, much more flexible, and capable of much greater effects.

Hopkins quite frequently composes according to the 'ordinary system', the normal basic iambic movement in English verse, what he later calls 'running rhythm', but there is no doubt that the bulk of his finest poetry is in sprung rhythm. His claim that it is more flexible is clearly true for him—the proof of the poem is in the reading. Moreover, he claims elsewhere that sprung rhythm 'is the native and natural rhythm of *speech*, the least forced, the most rhetorical and emphatic of all possible rhythms'. Hopkins's poetry is direct, usually spoken in the first person and normally dramatically very intense. It is a great advantage for poetry of such intensity that it should be able to contain whole series of stresses almost unrelieved by light syllables (slack),

e.g.   Súrf, snów, ríver and eárth
                    Gnáshed . . .

B

Here we have four stresses with only two syllables of slack in preparation for a fifth stress 'gnashed' at the beginning of the following line upon which the voice falls with all the ferocity it can command. Children do not need teaching that

díng, dóng, béll

controls the timing of

pússy's ín the wéll.

They know without question that the lines require the same time in the speaking. Where stresses in sequence are very powerful the natural pauses between them take, as it were, the place of light syllables. A similar discipline governs those sonnets of Hopkins that are written in sprung rhythm (*The Windhover* is a particularly good example of disciplined timing). It is of the first importance to remember that the flexibility that Hopkins has at his command brings with it a corresponding firmness and fineness of control. I think it is fair to say that the discipline is more demanding than that required for verse according to the 'ordinary system'.

Sprung rhythm for Hopkins discouraged the use of 'slack' as a kind of filling-in of the line. The result is a greater compression of language and this is what Hopkins normally aims at. If one turns to Tennyson, for example, after reading a poem of Hopkins one finds that his verse appears to be diluted. In taking advantage of the tightness of sprung rhythm Hopkins goes further in achieving compression by frequently imposing a strain on grammatical structure. Relative pronouns, conjunctions, even verbs are quite often omitted in the interest of energetic expression. Examples will be dealt with later, when individual poems are under consideration. Difficulties of interpretation, sometimes serious ones, arise from these omissions. Hopkins himself received a shock on re-reading parts of *The Loss of the Eurydice*:

> Everybody cannot be expected to like my pieces. Moreover the oddness may make them repulsive at first and yet Lang might have liked them on a second reading. Indeed when, on somebody returning me the *Eurydice*, I opened and read some lines, reading, as one commonly reads whether prose or verse, with the eyes, so to say, only, it struck me aghast with a kind of raw nakedness and unmitigated violence I was unprepared for . . .

No poet in English rewards more fully the closest application on the part of the reader. On first acquaintance the more complex poems may seem clotted, like lumpy porridge. Once the rhetorical order is perceived the pieces normally fall into place and the difficulties are forgotten.

Turn now to Hopkins's favourite verse form, the sonnet. Out of the forty-nine complete poems written in maturity between 1876 and 1889, thirty-four are in sonnet form. If we exclude eight inferior poems, it becomes clear how strong a hold the sonnet had on this poet. Apart from the metrical intricacy of *The Wreck of the Deutschland* the handling of the sonnet is the main evidence of Hopkins's technical virtuosity. Although it is not fashionable to discuss formal aspects of poetry nowadays, it would be unwise to neglect Hopkins's comments on his favourite verse form. He didn't think of the sonnet as a closed, fixed form, a cold mould waiting for the poet to fill, but as having potentialities unrealized in English. In the course of a discussion of the sonnet in a letter to Canon Dixon he praises the perfection of the Petrarchan sonnet as written in Italian, and proceeds to account for the slightness of the sonnet, with notable exceptions, in English. He finds that 'An Italian heroic line then and consequently a sonnet will be longer than an English in the proportion 13 : 10, which is considerable.' He enumerates devices successfully used to overcome this limitation, if the English sonnet is not to be 'light, tripping and trifling', and then goes on to say, 'it seems to me that for a mechanical difficulty the most mechanical remedy is the best: none, I think, meet it so well as these 'outriding' feet I sometimes myself employ, for they more than equal the Italian elisions and make the whole sonnet rather longer, if anything, than the Italian is. Alexandrine lines (used throughout) have the same effect'. The systematic use of 'outriders', extra-metrical feet, is characteristic of Hopkins in his sonnet writing. When he uses the word 'mechanical' he is clearly writing as a craftsman who wants to develop the medium in which he is working. A glance at *Spelt from Sybil's Leaves* will be sufficient to establish how far removed in some respects Hopkins's work was from the common run of contemporary sonnets. As in French sonnets it is written in Alexandrines, six stresses to the line, worked out under a very severe control, but, of course, unlike the French in its sprung rhythm basis. Hopkins wrote a number of orthodox sonnets on the Petrarchan model and even when extending the line and employing sprung rhythm he still sticks closely to the Petrarchan pattern, observing the break after the octave and employing an orthodox rhyme scheme. The ingenuity of his rhyming which is made acceptable not to the eye but in the process of declamation shows that even when the boldness of his experiment stretches the possibilities of the form to the limit, the original, basic Petrarchan conception is never lost sight of.

4

Before turning to a more detailed examination of the poetry it will be as well to remind ourselves of several more general considerations governing the kind of poetry Hopkins wrote.

In his own eyes Hopkins was first of all a priest. His art always took second place to his vocation; for him it was a marginal activity. He persistently refused the offices of his poet friend Canon Dixon in arranging for the publication of individual poems. He burnt, so he tells us, all the poetry that he could lay hands on written before he became a priest. He was encouraged by the Rector at St. Beuno's to write poetry again and *The Wreck of the Deutschland* was the outcome. Although while at Stonyhurst he appears to have experienced less sympathetic direction, his later appointment to the Chair of Greek at the Catholic University in Dublin, points to a genuine concern for Hopkins's peculiar gifts. It is wise to regard his poetry as a bye-product of the vocation of his choice, a choice he never regretted. The purity and honesty of his poetry reflect the unswerving dedication to his calling. There is evidence to show that in pursuit of perfection he imposed strains upon himself exceeding those laid upon him by his order.

It is important to stress the impressive fusion of his vocation and his artistry in the face of critical comment that suggests an opposition between the two. To give one example: T. S. Eliot in *After Strange Gods* sees Hopkins as essentially a Victorian nature poet and associates him with Meredith:

> Hopkins is not a religious poet in the more important sense in which I have elsewhere maintained Baudelaire to be a religious poet; or in the sense in which I consider Mr. Joyce's work to be penetrated with Christian feeling. I do not wish to depreciate him, but to affirm limitations and distinctions. He should be compared, not with our contemporaries whose situation is different from his, but with the minor poet nearest contemporary to him, and most like him: George Meredith. The comparison is altogether to Hopkins's advantage. They are both English nature poets, they have similar technical tricks and, Hopkins is much the more agile.
>
> (*After Strange Gods*, p. 48).

One can only say that the judgment is superficial. Hopkins's view of the natural world rests upon seeing it in all its aspects as evidence of the divine nature. The particulars of nature, however minute, are worthy of the closest inspection because they are eloquent of their creator. There is, indeed, only one purely nature-poem, *Inversnaid* in the body of his mature poetry. Even such poems as *Hurrahing in Harvest* and *The Windhover* are not primarily nature poems although they take their origin in moments of heightened awareness of aspects of the natural world. Many of the poems are concerned with man and his predicament in a natural world that he is in process of destroying. Every twig, every leaf is worthy of reverence because it offers evidence of divine energy.

Hence Hopkins's concern with inscape. Every particular in nature has its significant line. To grasp this essential form, which is the result of a pressure within the object to be what it is and not something else, is to increase awareness of the dappled, infinite variety and eccentricity of man's universe. There is a moving note written at Stonyhurst when an ash tree in the garden was cut down:

> April 8—The ashtree growing in the corner of the garden was felled. It was lopped first: I heard the sound and looking out and seeing it maimed there came at that moment a great pang and I wished to die and not to see the inscapes of the world destroyed any more.
>
> (Journal, 1873).

Nor is Hopkins's view of nature a simple, idealizing one. The above note is followed by the description of a dying ram:

> April 17—To Whitewell with Mr. Clarke. Saw a shoal of salmon in the river and many hares on the open hills. Under a stone hedge was a dying ram: there ran slowly from his nostril a thick flesh-coloured ooze, scarlet in places, coiling and roping its way down, so thick that it looked like fat.

The 'gnashing' of the elements in *The Wreck of the Deutschland* is sufficient evidence of Hopkins's sense of the darker mystery of God's will active in the natural world.

Above all, Hopkins is the poet of energy. Images of fire abound in his work: fire 'breaking from', fire 'flashing from'; nature seen as a bonfire forever burning. The inscapes of the poems themselves are evidence of creative energy: the strong bounding line of each poem is the result of the inner pressure that is driving it to take that form and no other.

Suggested Reading

Hopkins—The Journals and Papers, ed. Humphrey House and Graham Storey, Oxford University Press, 1959. (Study closely Hopkins's drawings, Notebooks and Journals.)

Ideas and Beliefs of the Victorians, Sylvan Press, 1949. (Read appropriate articles, particularly those on man and nature.)

Apologia Pro Vita Sua, J. H. Newman.

Modern Painters, Ruskin (Vol. 1, Section III, Ch. 1, Of Truth of Skies, and Ch. 11 of Truth of Clouds.

All in Due Time, Humphrey House (pp. 75–179), Rupert Hart-Davies, 1955.

Questions

1. Most readers find initial difficulties when beginning a study of Hopkins's poetry: would you say that these arise from the matter or the manner of the poems?

2. With which poems would you introduce the poetry of Hopkins to someone who knew nothing of the poet or his work? What advice would you give him to further his appreciation of Hopkins's poetry?

3. What do you think that Hopkins meant when he said that 'the poetical language of an age should be the current language heightened'?

4. 'We do not speak that way' Hopkins writes of the use of archaisms. Apply this dictum to Hopkins's own poetry.

5. Read Wordsworth's 'Preface to *Lyrical Ballads*' (1802 edition) and then write a dialogue between Hopkins and Wordsworth about poetic diction.

ST. BEUNO'S, N. WALES, 1874-7

1875	The Wreck of the Deutschland	
	The Silver Jubilee	
	Penmaen Pool, Barmouth	
1877	God's Grandeur	(Sonnet)
	The Starlight Night	(Sonnet)
	Spring	(Sonnet)
	In the Valley of the Elwy	(Sonnet)
	The Sea and the Skylark	(Sonnet)
	The Windhover	(Sonnet)
	Pied Beauty	(Curtal[1] Sonnet)
	Hurrahing In Harvest	(Sonnet)
	The Caged Skylark	(Sonnet)
	The Lantern Out of Doors	(Sonnet)

[1] Curtal = bob-tailed. A curtal sonnet, one of twelve lines instead of the usual fourteen, i.e., one with its tail docked.

The achieved poetry of Hopkins falls naturally into three
phases: the first, including *The Wreck of the Deutschland*
and a group of sonnets, covers the poet's stay at St.
Beuno's in North Wales; the second includes poems written at various times and places, less certain in mood and
direction; the third those poems written in Ireland, the
tragic phase. It will be convenient to treat the poetry
under these three heads. The first and third phases mark
themselves off very clearly, the second looks both backwards and forwards and presents less of a unity of effect.

Hopkins entered the Jesuit Order in 1868. From then
on until 1875, or possibly late December 1874, he wrote
no poetry apart from two or three sets of devotional
verse. When, in August 1874, he went to St. Beuno's in
North Wales to study theology, he almost immediately
determined to learn Welsh. After some hesitation he did
take lessons and attained sufficient command of the
language to write two poems in Welsh, one undated, the
other dated by W. H. Gardner as belonging to 1876. It is
doubtful whether after less than a year's study of Welsh
he would know sufficient about Welsh verse forms for
The Wreck of the Deutschland to owe much to them. It is
significant that in describing sprung rhythm he uses
exclusively English examples of it. There may have been
some Welsh influence upon his later poetry but there is
little in his verse practice that hasn't precedents in English

poetry. His knowledge of the complexities of Welsh forms no doubt gave some encouragement to the ingenuity and daring of his verse.

Whatever his debts may have been to Welsh poetry, there is no questioning the importance of his stay at St. Beuno's of over two years. He found in the Welsh landscape a paradisal freshness that became a source of the deepest inspiration to him. It would appear from *The Wreck of the Deutschland* that he had achieved a point in his vocation where, after conflict and suffering, he had triumphantly come through. The Welsh landscape called out to the poet as to a man new-born. The ecstatic quality of the poetry of the Welsh period reflects a harmony of relationships through which an internal spiritual bouyancy encouraged delight in the natural world, and the natural world, in its turn yielding its moments of revelation, reinforced the spiritual achievement. That is not to say that the poetry of this period is completely untroubled, but the vision is bright and a confident poise maintained.

Although *The Wreck of the Deutschland* was regarded by Bridges as the dragon at the gate, it will be as well to begin with a consideration of it. At the time of its composition Hopkins was studying theology at the Catholic house of St. Beuno's. The seminary stands on a hillside, hidden among the trees, at Tremeirchion, not far from St. Asaph. It occupies a superb natural setting, the front looks out over the Vale of Clywdd with the sea beyond, the back lies under the shadow of a rounded hill, 'the barrow of dark Maenefa the mountain'. The bedroom windows of the priests in training mostly look out either towards the sea or on to the mountain. The contrast between the austerity of the interior and the exuberance of the vegetation is dramatic. The formal terrace in front of the house and the terraced path leading from the main building to the ascent to the Rock Chapel whose slender spire as seen from the road is the only pointer to the existence of St. Bueno's, gives ample opportunity for a leisurely absorption of impressions of trees, landscape, sky and distant sea. Here 'on a pastoral forehead of Wales' Hopkins wrote *The Wreck of the Deutschland*.

2

This, the first of his mature poems, is marked by an unhesitating confidence. The hint from his rector that 'he wished someone would write a poem on the subject' was taken up with an enthusiasm that produced a poem unrivalled in the language for rhetorical power and intricacy. The immediate occasion for the poem was the wreck in the mouth of the Thames of the steamship *Deutschland*, with five Franciscan nuns on board. Hopkins's sources were the newspaper accounts in *The Times* and the *Illustrated London News*. The quality of the reporting is of an unusually high standard, marked by restrained vividness, compassion and lack of sensationalism. As we would expect, Hopkins dealt with the particulars faithfully and, it is worth remarking, the behaviour of the five nuns was singled out for admiration by *The Times* reporter, so that Hopkins cannot be charged with exaggerating their courage because they were co-religionists. The following extracts will give some idea of the material that he had to work on. The first two are descriptive of the wreck:

The Times, Thursday, December 9th, 1875
(The *Deutschland* ran aground on Monday, December 6th, at 5 a.m. *The Times* is quoting a survivor's account.)

The steamer struck on Monday morning at 5 o'clock. The sea was very rough, blowing hard from the east-north-east, thick with snow. The lead was cast every half-hour. We found 24 fathoms and then 17 fathoms. Immediately afterwards she struck, ship going dead slow. The engines were turned full speed astern, and immediately lost the propeller.... Two boats were lowered ... but both filled. No other boats were launched, the sea being too rough, but the rest were kept in readiness. Ultimately, however, the sea stove in and washed overboard the whole of the boats. During Monday, efforts were made by throwing cargo overboard, to keep the ship's stern to the sea . . . to prevent her getting broadside to the sea and passengers were sheltered, as far as possible, in the deck houses. The pumps were kept going all the day till dusk came on at 4 p.m. As the tide rose and the dark came on, the passengers and crew were compelled to take to the rigging. For the decks became awash.

The narrative continues on Saturday, December 11th:

But Monday was a tolerably clear day; passing vessels were distinctly seen from the *Deutschland*'s deck, and every effort was made to attract their attention. The passengers and crew watched these vessels, two of them steamers, hoping that each of them had seen or must soon see, the signal of distress. But one after another passed by and night came on. All this time the passengers had not suffered materially.... But after the first shock they kept up their spirits well. Plenty to eat and drink was served out to them, and the work to which the male passengers were put was useful in diverting their thoughts, but it became known that at night the rising tide and rough sea would imperil all on board. At night, therefore, rockets were thrown up once more, and this time they were answered from . . . a lightship to the south of the wreck . . . repeated at the Cork lightship and after some time they were answered by the coast guard at Harwich (27 miles away). . . . At 2 a.m. Captain Brickenstein knowing that with the rising tide the ship would be waterlogged, ordered all passengers to come on deck. . . . Most of them obeyed at once, . . . some of the ill, weak, despairing of life even on deck, resolved to stay in their cabins and meet death without any further struggle to evade it. At 3 a.m. on Tuesday morning a scene of horror was witnessed. Some passengers clustered for safety within or upon the wheelhouse, and on top of other slight structures on deck. Most of the crew and many of the emigrants went into the rigging, where they were safe enough as long as they could maintain their hold. But the intense cold and long exposure told a tale. The purser of the ship, though a strong man, relaxed his hold and fell into the sea. Women and children and men were one by one swept away from their shelters on the deck. Five German nuns, whose bodies are now in the dead-house here, clasped hands and were drowned together, the chief sister, a gaunt woman 6 feet high, calling out loudly and often 'O Christ, come quickly!' till the end came. The shrieks and sobbing of women and children are described by the survivors as agonizing. One brave sailor, who was safe in the rigging, went down to try and save a child or woman who was drowning on deck. He was secured by a rope to the rigging but a wave dashed him against the bulwarks, and when daylight dawned his headless body, detained by the rope, was seen swaying to and fro with the waves. In the dreadful excitement of these hours, one man hung himself behind the wheelhouse, another hacked at his wrist with a knife, hoping to die a comparatively painless death by bleeding. It was nearly 8 o'clock before the tide and sea abated and the survivors could venture to go on deck. At half past 10 o'clock the tugboat from Harwich came alongside and brought away all without further accident.

The third extract is an account of the preparations for the burial of the five nuns. The wreck, it is to be noted, was of sufficient significance to the Catholic community for Cardinal Manning to give the funeral oration.

The Times. Monday, December 13th

Four of the five nuns who perished by the wreck are to be buried at Leytonstone to-day. They belonged to a Franciscan nunnery in Westphalia, and are regarded by their co-religionists in London as having been exiled from their native land in consequence of the Falck Laws. When their deaths became known it was resolved by the Authorities of the Roman Catholic Church in London to give the bodies solemn burial. For this purpose two Franciscan Fathers were dispatched to Harwich, and the bodies were placed in oak coffins lined with white satin and brought to London on Friday evening. On reaching Stratford they were delivered over to the care of the nuns of the Convent of Jesus and Mary, who, assisted by the nuns of the Sacred Heart, prepared their dead sisters for burial.

The dead nuns were wearing, with slight variation, the dress common to the order; and as there was found on each dress the number assigned to a nun in making her profession of religion, all will, no doubt, in this way be identified. After being made ready the bodies lay in state in the spacious school-room below the Franciscan Church at Stratford throughout Saturday and yesterday. The open coffins lay side by side upon a raised dais, lighted candles were placed beside the coffins, while vases of flowers and wreaths of immortelles were grouped at the heads and feet. Upon both days large numbers of people visited the place, the major portion of whom appeared to be prompted by feelings of devotion. The deceased appeared to be between the ages of thirty and forty and their faces wore an expression of calmness and resignation. Their fingers were clasped upon a rosary and crucifix; upon the breast of each lay a cross of white flowers, the gifts of the Ursuline nuns of Upton. One, noted for her extreme tallness, is the lady who, at midnight on Monday, by standing on a table in the Saloon, was able to thrust her body through the skylight, and kept exclaiming, in a voice heard by those in the rigging above the roar of the storm 'My God, my God, make haste, make haste'. There will be a solemn Mass in the Franciscan Church at eleven this morning. Cardinal Manning will deliver a funeral oration over the deceased, after which they will be interred in St. Patrick's Catholic Cemetery, Leytonstone.

Turning to the poem we see that of its thirty-five stanzas only nine are fully given to the narrative of the wreck. The proportion of narrative to meditative and lyrical elements provides a clue to its character. Hopkins in a letter to Bridges describes it 'as an ode and not primarily narrative'. That being so, consider the relationship of the first to the second part of the poem.

There is no specific reference to the *Deutschland* in the first part of the poem. It opens with an address in the first person to God, acknowledging his mastery and all-sustaining power. There follows a moving evocation of the poet's suffering and triumph in relating himself to the working of God's will, in the course of which experience he had been on the point of annihilation. The release from exhausting spiritual and physical tension is expressed ecstatically at first in the great, mounting rhythm of:

> I whirled out wings that spell
> And fled with a fling of the heart to the heart of the Host.
> My heart, but you were dovewinged, I can tell,
> Carrier-witted, I am bold to boast,
> To flash from the flame to the flame then, tower from the grace to the grace.

and, then, more steadily in two stanzas in which Hopkins, sustained by Christ's gift, defines his contentment, first in the hour-glass image, the sand moving effortlessly with the pull of gravity and then in the water-level-in-a-well image where the 'pane' of water is supported smooth, clear and steady by the underground streams that 'rope' it to the mountain. The account of the poet's satisfaction in his hardly-won vision is concluded in the fifth stanza where he greets stars, star-light ('wafting him out of it'), thunder and dappled sky. The passage from suffering to a sense of glory in the first part of the poem is balanced in the second by the anguish of the wreck giving way to the ecstasy of the nun. It provides a base upon which the structure of the interpretation of the working of God's will may securely rest. In a letter to Bridges written from St. Beuno's in August, 1877, Hopkins writes 'I may add for your greater interest and edification that what refers to myself in the poem is all *strictly* and *literally* true and *did all occur*; nothing is added for poetical padding' (my italics).

The remainder of the first part of the poem has to do with the working of God's will in man, predominantly as manifested in the stress to be endured. The stress (cf. 'laced with fire of stress', stanza 2) does not take its origin, we are told, in Christ's bliss but 'dates from day / Of his going in Galilee; . . . The dense and the driven Passion, and frightful sweat'. Man, then, may expect to come to a knowledge of God through an extremity of suffering. The suffering endured, however severe, is to be welcomed if man as 'rebel, dogged in den' is to be saved. God may make himself manifest on occasion in another mode 'stealing as Spring through him' but, whatever the fashion of it, man must praise God for his ultimate care:

> Father and fondler of heart thou hast wrung:
> Hast thy dark descending and most art merciful
>   then.

There are certain obscurities in stanzas 4, 5 and 6 which cannot be explored here. My primary aim has been to indicate the direction the poem is taking in the first part in order to bring out its bearing upon the second. The desperate plight, his own, that the poet so dramatically images in stanzas 2 and 3 is paralleled by that of the nuns, and even the worse plight of the 'unconfessed of them' in the second part. The violence of the verbs 'sweep', 'hurl', 'trod' is a preparation for the even more anguished vein of the narrative of the wreck when in stanza 13 'sweeps' and 'hurling' are again used. 'Stroke and stress that stars and storms deliver' is an obvious preparation for what is to come. 'Hast thy dark descending' is echoed in the later 'dark side of the bay of thy blessing'. And in stanza 9 of the first part the poet adjures God to 'Wring thy rebel, dogged in den, / Man's malice, with *wrecking and storm*'. The theme of the poem is contained in the central paradox:

> Beyond saying sweet, past telling of tongue,
> Thou art lightning and love, I found it, a winter
> and warm; . . .

The alternating movement from apparently cruel and terrifying pressures to a sense of release in pure joy that characterises the first part is to be repeated in the second in the dramatic re-creation of the circumstances of the wreck upon which the ecstatic variations are then played, matching the opening and concluding stanzas of Part the First.

The second part of the poem opens with Death beating out the names of the agents of violent death on his drum, and, the poet adds, 'storms bugle his fame', as though death were announcing an assault by his legion upon the living. But we, the living, behave as though unconscious of death's approach even though we are of the same stuff as those who are falling within sight of us, forgetting that the same scythe is for us too. 'Cringe' in the last line of this stanza suggests not only the low sweep of the scythe but the grass bowing before it, a wincing of the body.

There follows the magnificent imaginative re-creation

of the wreck, unrivalled in English narrative verse for power and accuracy. The account continues for five stanzas when it is interrupted by the parenthetical stanza 18 which is introduced at the point where the voice of the tall nun is heard, 'a virginal tongue told'. It is an important but difficult stanza, for in a sense it determines the direction the poem is to take from this point onwards. It reflects an agitated response to the situation with the poet first of all registering the compulsion to cry out in pain from the centre of his being and to utter words of truth (in spite of a predisposition to evil), and to weep. But the weeping, far from being painful, is 'a melting, a madrigal start! . . . What can it be, this glee?'; the reply is only hinted at in the further question: Can it be 'the good you have there of your own?' I presume the 'your own' refers to the 'heart's good', the re-discovery of the 'heart's good' through the medium of the nun. Interpretation is not made any easier by the perplexing sixth line. Whatever the exact implication of this stanza the reader is shocked (and intended to be surprised) by the tones of 'madrigal start' and 'this glee' both expressive of unrestrained joy—a mood as remote as possible from that of the preceding stanza ('They fought with God's cold'). The paradox is not verbal but lies in the experience itself. When the torment is most acute, joy is released.

When the narrative resumes the nun is firmly established as the centre of it. She is represented as calling on Christ: though blinded by the breaking seas, she *sees* her one objective; her voice is heard above the storm's confusion, calling on 'her master'. Observe that although the 'virginal tongue' is introduced in stanza 17, it is not until stanza 24 that her words 'O Christ, Christ, come quickly' enter the poem. Before this point is reached Hopkins gives the background of the five nuns, that they are on the *Deutschland* because they have been banned from their homeland for their beliefs. And in spite of what man and the elements can do to them, Christ (Orion of light, i.e. as hunter of souls) is above, in whose sight the 'storm flakes' are 'lily-showers'. There follows an improvisation on the fact of there being five nuns, treated by Hopkins as a sign that they have been specially favoured even as St. Francis was favoured by receiving the stigmata. At this point (stanza 24) Hopkins compares his own security at the time of the wreck with the plight of the nuns, the better to bring out the full force of the tall nun's 'O Christ, Christ, come quickly'. In calling on the crucified Christ in her extremity her 'wild-worst' condition is christened 'Best'. What did she mean by her words? Hopkins offers two possible interpretations in the form of questions but before rejecting them he evokes a transformation in the natural world as the 'down-dugged ground-hugged grey / Hovers off' to reveal the jay-blue, May sky. The transformation of the physical universe is in itself a kind of miracle and prepares the way for the rhetorically daring twenty-eighth stanza. Here the poet with a perhaps too obvious artifice mimics through broken verbal gestures his closing in on the heart of the matter, the nun's aware-ness of the presence of Christ himself. Her single-minded-ness has earned its reward, appropriately enough on the eve of the feast of the Immaculate Conception. But what of the others, 'the unconfessed of them'? Surely the nun by her example and intervention might be a means of bringing the stray sheep back: '. . . is the shipwrack then a harvest, does tempest carry the grain for thee?'

The poet returns to the theme of the mastery and mys-tery of God (32), to the mercy and compassion of Christ, to the vision of a visitation refreshing as a shower of rain 'not a lightning of fire hard-hurled' (cf. stanza 10, 'stealing as Spring'). There follows a prayer to the nun, that her intervention may be the means of bringing Christ back to 'rare-dear Britain', and the poem ends with the majestic, mounting rhythms that celebrate the centrality of Christ in the poet's universe.

The Wreck of the Deutschland is a poem remarkable in its consistency, all the more so as Hopkins had abandoned the practice of poetry for some years before its composition. The virtuosity with which he handles his eight-line stanza, peculiarly his own invention, providing as it does a maximum of metrical freedom with a quite stern over-all control, places him among the great masters of English verse. The verse pattern is maintained through both parts of the poem, with the exception of one modification in the second part where the first line of each stanza is strengthened: three main stresses instead of two are employed. It would seem to me that in the first part it is possible, even desirable, to allow three stresses in the first line of certain stanzas:

e.g.   Thou mastering me God

> (Mr. W. H. Gardner would give a secondary stress on 'mastering' but as the theme is God's mastery this seems to weaken the effect.)

or again, I find it difficult not to stress the 'I' in

'I am soft sift'.

It seems probable that Hopkins, feeling the need for a stronger first line, regularized the three-stress pattern in the second part of the poem.

The regular stress pattern is 2 or 3 (first line), 3, 4, 3, 5, 5, 4, 6. The progression to the final alexandrine (six-stress line) is marked by a steady lengthening of the line broken by the interposition of a three-stress fourth line and a four-stress seventh line. The reinforcing of stress by alliteration is capable of producing unusual power and such verse, in the reading aloud, makes a considerable physical demand on the reader. The following stanza illustrates as well as any the resourcefulness of Hopkins in exploiting stress, rhyme and alliteration.

Stresses		*Rhyme*
3	Loathed for a Love men knew in them,	a
3	Banned by the land of their Birth	b
4	Rhine Refused them, Thames would Ruin them;	
		a
3	Surf, Snow, river and earth	b
5	Gnashed: but thou art above, thou Orion of	
	light;	c
5	Thy unchancelling Poising Palms were	
	Weighing the Worth,	b
4	Thou Martyr-Master: in thy Sight	c
6	Storm Flakes were Scroll-leaved Flowers,	
	lily Showers-Sweet heaven was aStrew in them.	
		a

The rhyme scheme is maintained as assiduously throughout the poem as the stress-system. There is no deviation from it at any point. This is all the more impressive as the stanza depends on three rhymes only, two of which, 'a' and 'b', are used three times. How insistent Hopkins always was on formal correctness to the point of eccentric rhyming is even more evident in some of the later sonnets, e.g. *Spelt from Sibyl's Leaves*. The ingenuity by which Hopkins meets his metrical contract is shown in stanza 31 where after 'rest *of them*' comes 'unconfessed *of them*' to be followed by 'the breast *of the* | *M*aiden'— the rhyme completed at the beginning of the following line. When read with the ear or declaimed the rhyme works well enough although it looks rather strange to the eye.

Two other points about the rhyme scheme are worthy of attention: the first, that the initial rhyme is also the last. Each stanza tends to have a certain completeness of its own even while it is serving the larger design of the work and this effect is reinforced by the rhyming of the first and last lines. (Bear in mind, too, that the last line is always an alexandrine, carrying six stresses often of unusual weight). In the first part of the poem only two stanzas (7 and 8) are linked by the running-over of one into the other. In the second part there is no running-over unless the transition from stanza 32 to 33 is counted as such, but in this instance stanza 32 ends with a semi-colon and comes to rest with a long, contented pause before the movement resumes.

But while each stanza has something of a self-containedness, a quality appropriate to the mood of excited meditation that governs the poem, it also makes itself felt as a link in a sequence that is essentially dramatic. The dramatic immediacy of the poem derives, of course, from the sustained rhythmic energy, the capacity to screw up tensions within the stanza and to relax pressure at will; from the active vocabulary, (note the high proportion of vigorous verbs and of verbs used as nouns); the skilful use of tense, the easy transition from an immediate past to a vivid present (cp. stanza 1) to achieve the effect of the past not only realized in the present but of *the past's significance* in process of revelation as the poem advances. The whole range of rhetorical devices, the dramatic questionings, exclamations, desperate repetitions ('where was a, where was a place?'), the apostrophising of Christ, the nuns, Father Francis, etc., all move the reader to take up the position of the poet. The Van Gogh-like energy sucks the reader into the vivid, impetuous movement.

Many of the superficial difficulties of Hopkins's verse disappear with familiarity. Because he always writes for the speaking voice, the punctuation will be found to help with breathing and in assessing the appropriate length of pauses. His grammar is that of speech rather than of the printed word. But difficulties do remain, however familiar one is with the poem. There are the obscurities that arise when the grammatical structure is not clear (cf. stanza 6), but there are also dark patches in the poem that derive from the nature of the subject. The poet is wrestling to make available experience of a kind not normally accessible, that can only be expressed by hints and suggestions. On the other hand in a letter to Bridges in May, 1878, Hopkins says that he was 'not over-desirous that the meaning of all should be quite clear'. No doubt there are implications in the poem obvious to a scholarly catholic that will be passed over by those of us who are not of that faith. Whether Hopkins was deliberately veiling his meaning in a degree that would seriously affect consistent interpretation of the poem is very doubtful.

3

The Wreck of the Deutschland was finished by the end of June 1876 for by that time Hopkins was submitting it for publication to the Jesuit magazine, *The Month*. By the end of September it had not appeared and Hopkins knew that it had been rejected. Apart from the fragment *Moonrise*, interesting for its precise St. Beuno's setting as well as for its quality, a set of devotional verses, *The Silver Jubilee*, of no particular merit, and the occasional verses of *Penmaen Pool*, Hopkins appears to have written almost nothing until February 1877 when *God's Grandeur* was composed. There followed a productive burst that lasted until September of that year. All the poems, ten of them, are sonnets and among them are some of his best and most characteristic pieces.

The dominant theme in this group of sonnets is the ecstatic celebration of the natural world, its freshness, its splendid and varied energies. Over against this purity the poet expresses his sense of human deficiency, of man's falling short, his unworthiness in this paradisal context, and to a lesser degree, his role as despoiler. The divine energy (instress) is seen as manifesting itself through natural forms: hence through nature man may sense the creator.

In several of the sonnets the ecstatic delight in nature and the consciousness of human estrangement from it are presented in contrast. *God's Grandeur* begins with an assertion of a world charged with divine energy. Hopkins gives expression to his sense of this in two images. Of the first, 'it will flame out, like shining from shook foil', Hopkins's note tells us:

I mean foil in its sense of leaf or tinsel, and no other
word whatever will give the effect I want. Shaken gold-
foil gives off broad glares like sheet lightning and also,
... owing to its zigzag dints and creasings and network
of small many-cornered facets, a sort of fork lightning
too.

The image is one of considerable and exact complexity
suggesting both at the same time a dazzling, many-
faceted play of light, 'shook' giving the vibratory quality.
The second image 'it gathers to a greatness, like the
ooze of oil crushed,' is not as simple as it looks. Presumably it is derived from the oil-press, the crushing of
olives, or of oil-bearing seeds. The squeezing out of the
essential juices may be seen as relating to their precious
quality and hence to the in-dwelling divine energy; 'the
gathering to a greatness', the oil no longer existing in
individual seeds or olives, but flowing or bulging out
under pressure. Thus the 'ooze of oil' stands in relation
to its source in nature as 'the flaming out' does to the
shook foil; in the variety there is a compelling unity; the
world is so charged. Following immediately on the two
images the poet asks: Why, in the face of this grandeur of
God flaming out, 'do men, ... not reck his rod?' Then
in a succession of powerful verbs *seared* (with trade) ...
bleared, smeared (with toil) and evocative nouns *smudge* and
smell, Hopkins declares the disharmony between man
and nature. A whole train of images presents man as both
defiled and defiling. His senses are blunted, his shoes
even are barriers between himself and the life-giving
earth. But for all his efforts that defile, 'nature is never
spent;'. However dark the outlook, the poet ends the
sonnet in the comfort of his knowledge that the Holy

Ghost is brooding over the 'bent' world. 'Bent', I take it, suggests the curving of the earth's surface, and possibly, includes the world of man, his deformity and despoilation of the earth.

A similar disharmony is expressed in *The Valley of the Elwy* and *The Sea and the Skylark*. *The Valley of the Elwy* depends for its interpretation on Hopkins's extraneous comment and is, therefore, an unsatisfactory poem. Its title suggests that the remembered house of the first line is in the valley. Not so!—'the kind people of the sonnet were the Watsons of Shooter's Hill'. To the uninitiated the octave of the sonnet suggests a particularly satisfying harmony between man and nature. Human relationships are expressed in nature's language:

> That cordial air made those kind people a hood
> All over, as a bevy of eggs the mothering wing
> Will, or mild nights the new morsels of Spring:
> Why, it seemed of course; seemed of right it should.

The lines that follow are in harmony with the foregoing:

> Lovely the woods, waters, meadows, combes, vales,
> All the air things wear that build this world of Wales . . .

And then, much to the reader's surprise (for he doesn't know about those exceptional people of Shooter's Hill or that such people are not to be found in Wales!) 'Only the inmate does not correspond': Too much has to be supplied for the poem to make immediate sense but once we are in the know, the poem gathers a true significance: in this Welsh paradise the inmate, man, alone fails to match. It is to be noted that the last three lines of the sonnet hark back to the *Deutschland* in 'swaying considerate scales', a subdued echo of 'unchancelling poising palms'; 'being a father and fond', of 'father and fondler' (stanza 9).

The Sea and the Skylark written at Rhyl presents the nature/state-of-man contrast in a particularly successful, formal manner. The octave is given to the contrasting sounds of breaking sea and song of the lark ascending. The song of the lark is elaborately and energetically defined in Hopkins's own commentary on a slightly different earlier version: '*Rash fresh more* . . . means a headlong and exciting new snatch of singing, resumption by the lark of his song, which by turns he gives over and takes up again all day long, and this goes on, the sonnet says, through all time, *without ever losing its first freshness,* . . .' (but see the full comment in letter to Bridges, Nov. 26, 1882). The ground-bass of the sea and the fragile variety of the lark's song will go on for ever without losing freshness while man, in the sestet, is put to shame by their purity. He has lost that 'cheer and charm of earth's past prime', is fast declining into the slime from which he came. The view of man, not only as a fallen creature but steadily deteriorating, is expressed in its most extreme form here and nature in all its freshness is used as the measure of that fall.

A sonnet to put alongside *the Sea and the Skylark* is the delightful slightly earlier *Spring* where the octave conveys to perfection the sense of a new birth, the weeds 'in wheels', the thrush-egg blue, bird-song, light on leaves, boughs brushing sky, all caught in an excited, delighted *rhythmic dance* of sustained energy. The sestet opens with a question related to what has gone before, supplies an answer, and to conclude commends to Christ the souls of children in their spring-time:

What is all this juice and all this joy?
   A strain of the earth's sweet being in the beginning
In Eden garden.—Have, get, before it cloy,
   Before it cloud, Christ, lord, and sour with sinning,
Innocent mind and Mayday in girl and boy,
   Most, O maid's child, thy choice and worthy the win-
      ning.

While the buoyancy of the mood pervades the whole sonnet, the gravity with which Hopkins introduces his
'before it cloy . . . cloud . . . and sour' immediately after
his reference to Eden garden, not only reminds us of the
Fall, but of the anticipated deterioration as in *The Sea and
the Skylark*. Only Christ's intervention, it would appear,
can prevent it.

To turn now to a group of three sonnets, written one
after the other, between May and September, 1877: *The
Windhover, Pied Beauty*, and *Hurrahing in Harvest*. All three
poems are ecstatic with an ecstasy derived from an
intense responsiveness to the natural world and sense of
God in or behind it. *Pied Beauty* expresses these qualities
in their most direct, untroubled form. It is a curtal sonnet
(has had its tail cut) and is written in sprung rhythm with
persistent alliteration. It is a short hymn of praise, a Te
Deum, in which the variety, individuality and contrasting
qualities in both the natural and in the man-made worlds
(the 'dappledness of things') are celebrated. The last line
contains the great paradox that God who fathers-forth
the transient and variegated universe is himself unchang-
ing. Much-anthologized as the poem has been, and
deservedly so, it is probably best read in the company of
poems written in the same year. Notice how beginning
with very precise images the poem goes on to suggest

in the last quatrain by means of twelve carefully selected, carefully related adjectives the central theme, and by their placing in a very tight and alert rhythmical order moves the poem to the powerful assertiveness of the last line. 'Rose-moles all in stipple' is an image typical of the directness and compression of Hopkins's images: 'rose' gives colour; 'mole' shape and size of spots of colour; 'stipple' their arrangement. 'Fresh-firecoal chestnut-falls' is usually taken to refer to the fallen chestnuts but '*fresh-fire*' would rather suggest the fallen blossom of the red-chestnut which when circling the tree from which it has dropped, has very much the appearance of live coals.

The Windhover has been so often analysed and been found to carry so many interpretations that one is tempted to hurry on without more ado. It is, I think, the most important poem to be written in this phase of Hopkins's life. In it he returns to the sustained use of sprung rhythm and develops it beyond the stage reached in the *Deutschland*. The octave has an extreme flexibility of verse which allows the poet to mimic the movements of the falcon: first in its effortless mastery as it rides the air; then in following the great swerving movement as it challenges and overcomes the wind. Here, if anywhere, the poet's advice—'take breath and read me with the ear' must be observed! Alliteration and stress work together superbly. The whole poem has such an air of confident control that it is surprising that it has been open to so many diverse interpretations. It is only possible here to point briefly to the difficulties, and to the reading that I favour.

The major difficulties lie in the sestet, but before we get to it 'my heart in hiding' prepares the way for them. If we relate 'my heart in hiding' to the opening 'I caught' we can appreciate the measure of impact at the sight of the falcon upon the poet. 'Caught' both suggests the glad surprise at the spectacle and the sense of coming upon the bird unobserved. All we can legitimately take from the 'in hiding' is that the inward-looking mind has been startled out of its withdrawnness; and, perhaps, 'for a bird' suggests how strange and wonderful that it should be so, that there should be such 'mastery' in one creature.

The first line of the sestet names in series the splendid attributes that are seen to be concentrated in the falcon. I take 'buckle' to mean 'come together', 'are here fastened together'. The word has been variously interpreted, for example, 'buckle' as applied to a bicycle wheel or as in 'buckle to'. The comma between 'plume' and 'here' is probably rhetorical, to ensure that 'plume' gets due weight. Up to this point I am convinced that the poem has to do with the bird and is not consciously symbolical or allegorical. Subsequently serious difficulties in interpretation arise. Why does the poet stress 'and'? Who or what is the 'thee' in 'the fire that breaks from thee then,'?

As we have seen, the dominant theme in the group of poems under discussion is the freshness of the natural world and the sense of God's grandeur shining out of it. In this respect these poems develop an important aspect of *The Wreck of the Deutschland* where the elements are seen as being involved in the working out of God's will; but closer to the key of these later poems is the stanza 'I kiss my hand / To the stars, lovely-asunder / Starlight, wafting him out of it'; If the 'him' (Christ) can be wafted out of the starlight, he must in some sense be there to be wafted. We have already seen that God's grandeur flames out of a world charged with him and in *Hurrahing in Harvest* the poet speaks of 'gleaning our

D

Saviour' in the cloudscape. Hopkins's consciousness of nature as a source of revelation, of God (Christ) active in the universe is so acute at this time that 'fire that breaks from *thee* then' would seem to me to refer to Christ. But does it refer to Christ in the windhover or to Christ by way of contrast with the bird? My view is that the poet first sees the windhover in flight and is increasingly possessed by it in his concentration of attention. The kestrel presents itself irresistibly as a miracle of disciplined energy until the point is reached when the divine energy may be said to break out of it. The accentuated '*and*' marks the sense of revelation. Once the windhover is experienced as being *charged* with Christ, the 'billion times told lovelier, more dangerous', follows quite naturally and 'O my chevalier!' now becomes Christ (in the windhover). On this reading the poet experiences a sudden glory, a moment of ecstatic recognition of the presence of Christ. I agree that the emphatic 'and' might be taken as dividing the physical splendour of the windhover from the infinite beauty of Christ but the relationship between 'chevalier' and 'dauphin' has not the same subtlety in this reading. The last three lines, too, offer some difficulty. I would summarize the argument as follows: the ploughshare suffers its own transformation— by daily use it, too, shines out; the dying fire with its deceptive, blue-cindery appearance, will open and reveal a sudden glory. The 'ah my dear' points to a weight of personal experience behind the images. Would it be going too far to suggest that the 'heart in hiding' is related to the daily toil and dedicated purpose (as of the ploughshare); that it has its reward in the moment of illumination with 'gash gold-vermilion' conveying both pain and glory?

Hurrahing in Harvest may be seen as a companion-piece to the *Windhover*. It was, Hopkins informs Bridges, the outcome of half an hour of extreme enthusiasm 'as I walked home alone one day from fishing in the Elwy'. The poet attempts to recapture in verse the exhilaration he has experienced by a dramatic use of the present tense —'Summer ends now; . . . the stooks arise . . . what lovely behaviour . . . I walk . . .'.—The octave is rich in harvest images: first the stooks, 'barbarous in beauty', suggesting an encamped army; then clouds, now like drifts of meal, now like silken sacks; and finally the powerful '*glean* our Saviour' image. The sprung rhythm has a matured flexibility. Observe how the poem has within its unity a four-part structure. The first four lines set the scene, relate the rising fields of stooked corn to a cloud-scape of warm, generous autumnal shapes and tones, rhetorically presented by means of the ejaculatory 'what! . . . what!' The movement is fluid, each line overflowing into the next and in doing so, not drawing attention to the extra-ordinary rhymes. The second movement with its dramatic progress of 'I walk, I lift up heart, eyes, / Down all that glory in the heavens . . .' is reminiscent of the psalmist's 'I will lift up mine eyes unto the hills from whence cometh my help'. What human love, asks the poet, ever gave so generous, so well-founded, a return? As the second quatrain of the octave is a response to the first, so in the sestet the images of the hills prepare the way for the final assertion of the ecstatic experience; once the receptive mind meets (greets and is greeted by) the natural world, the ecstasy knows no bounds in an uprush of pure energy ('heart rears wings') that almost overcomes the pull of the earth and dead-weight of the body.

The poem deserves much more detailed comment than

there is room for here. Three particulars may be singled out for attention. The use of '*barbarous*' in the first line where the stress, coming heavily on 'barb', suggests in its context something like 'wild', 'exuberant' 'splendour', and also 'bristling', the spear-like formation of the stooks. '*Meal-drift moulded* . . .': 'meal-drift' on the model of snowdrift; 'moulded' suggests the satisfying contours of meal drifting and gives a warmth and solidity to the image. '*Very-violet-sweet*': the violet light on the Welsh hills in combination with their muscular formation gives a happy fusion of strength and tenderness. The sky like an azure cloth is thrown over the hills or rather draped over them, filling in the gaps between.

The ecstatic vein in Hopkins's poetry is essentially related to his stay at St. Beuno's. One poem, the *Starlight Night*, consists for the most part of admiring ejaculations —'Look at the stars! . . . look! . . . look!' On September 23, 1877, he was ordained priest and a new phase in his life and poetry began.

Suggested Reading

The Letters of Gerard Manley Hopkins to Robert Bridges, Ed. C. C. Abbott, Oxford University Press, 1955.

The Wreck of the Deutschland, W. H. Gardner, Essays and Studies, No. 21, 1935.

The Wreck of the Deutschland, John E. Keating, Kent State University Bulletin, January 1963.

The Windhover, F. N. Lees, Scrutiny, Vol. XVII, No. 1, Spring 1950.

Gerard Manley Hopkins, a critical study, W. A. M. Peters, S.J., Oxford University Press, 1948. (Especially for discussion of 'inscape'.).

Immortal Diamond, Ed. Norman Weyand, S.J., Sheed & Ward, 1949 (for fuller reports of the wreck of the *Deutschland*).

Questions

1. Compare *Hurrahing in Harvest* with Keats's *Ode to Autumn*.

2. Illustrate and discuss the aspects of nature which particularly appeal to Hopkins and which he emphasizes in his poetry.

3. 'Hopkins is the poet of energy.' Illustrate from his poetry.

4. Discuss the argument that the difficulty of *understanding The Wreck of the Deutschland* prevents enjoyment and appreciation of the poem.

5. By what means does Hopkins secure his most striking effects in *The Wreck of the Deutschland*?

THE MIDDLE YEARS, 1878–1884

1878 *Derbyshire*
    The Loss of the Eurydice
    Stonyhurst
    The May Magnificat

1879 *Oxford*
    Binsey Poplars
    Duns Scotus's Oxford   (Sonnet)
    Henry Purcell   (Sonnet)
    The Candle Indoors   (Sonnet)
    The Handsome Heart   (Sonnet)
    The Bugler's First Communion
    Morning, Midday and Evening Sacrifice
    Andromeda   (Sonnet)
    Peace   (Curtal Sonnet)
    Bedford (Lancs.)
    At the Wedding March

1880 *Liverpool*
    Felix Randal   (Sonnet)
    Hampstead
    Brothers
    Lydiate (Lancs.)
    Spring and Fall

1881 *Inversnaid*
    Inversnaid
    As Kingfishers Catch Fire   (Sonnet)
    (Date and place of composition not precisely known.)

1882 *Stonyhurst*
    Ribblesdale   (Sonnet)
    The Leaden Echo and the Golden Echo

1883 The Blessed Virgin compared to the Air we Breathe.

Hopkins's ordination at the age of thirty-three, following on some ten years preparation, exposed him after a contemplative life to the rigours of parish work. He had hoped for a further year of theological study but this was denied him.

His first appointment was at Mount St. Mary's College, Chesterfield, where he remained until April 1878. His muse 'turned sullen in the Sheffield smoke-laden air'; *The Wreck of the Eurydice* was the only production during his stay there. In May he returned for a few months to Stonyhurst and in July he went for about three months to London to be select preacher at Mount Street where he remained until November. From London he moved to Oxford where at the parish church of St. Aloysius he served for the best part of a year, a period that produced a crop of some nine poems at fairly regular intervals.

The choice of place appeared to be admirable for his scholarly temperament but, whatever the sources of his uneasiness at Oxford, it would seem that he was transferred to north-country industrial parishes in accordance with his wishes. A stay of three months at Leigh in Lancashire was an encouragement to him and seemed to confirm his inclination. The people were warm, hearty, sympathetic and, above all, he felt that he was needed by them: 'It is sweet to be a little flattered . . . these Lancashire people of low degree or not of high degree are those who most seemed to me to welcome me and make much of me.' But his duties at Leigh were only temporary and after three months he was transferred to Liverpool. The experience was disastrous. St. Francis Xavier's was the kind of church where people came for the preaching and Hopkins, with his fastidious temperament, his small body, his high-pitched voice, was not equipped for the role of pulpit orator. He had to suffer the humiliation of being instructed to write his sermons and the indignity of the pasting-over on the printed bills of the title of his last sermon there, 'The Fall of God's First Kingdom': 'I was not allowed to take this title and on the printed bills it was covered by a blank slip pasted over.' One must allow that the sermons, fine as they often are, were not without their eccentricities. As a popular preacher in a fashionable pulpit Hopkins was out of place. What to do with such a man? Human institutions, however flexible, don't easily accommodate his like. To add to his distress at what he believed to be his failure in the pulpit was the more important impact of Liverpool's poverty and squalor. Long afterwards in the February before his death he wrote to Bridges: '. . . our whole civilisation is dirty, yea filthy, and especially in the north; for is it not dirty, yea filthy, to pollute the air as Blackburn and Widnes and St. Helens are polluted and the water as the Thames and the Clyde and the Irwell are polluted?' This passage follows on a description of a Liverpool street on a frosty morning 'starred with the spit of the workmen going to their work'. At the time of his great unhappiness in Liverpool, he could speak of 'remarking for the thousandth time with sorrow and loathing the base and bespotted figures and features of the Liverpool crowd'.

The parish work was 'wearying to body and mind' and it is not surprising that he only managed to write twenty-six lines of verse in the six months after leaving Oxford. When Hopkins left Liverpool he was to enter on the year of his tertianship at Roehampton, a period of taking stock, spiritual refreshment and the making of his last vows. We must constantly remind ourselves that he was before all else by vocation a priest and this was not a time for artistic creation. The evidence suggests that he emerged with renewed confidence, a reinforced dedication and with at least two poetic works in mind, a great ode on the Catholic martyr, Thomas Campion (lost, if ever written) and a play on the theme of St. Winefred. He was now to teach classics at Stonyhurst to young men who had finished their schooling but who were not able to enter Oxford or Cambridge. The appointment, one would imagine, should have been congenial. Unfortunately the Provincial, Father Purbrick, seems to have been of an administrative cast of mind that Hopkins found uncongenial. 'It was borne in on him,' writes Father Devlin, 'that he must look on his poetic genius as an amiable weakness which a hardworking Jesuit might indulge for an hour or two occasionally'—this at a time when he was in need of the most positive encouragement to fulfil his creative needs. Even though he had the leisure, he became depressed and was unable to use it. The *St. Winefred's Well* choruses and another fragment were nearly all he produced in the best part of two years at Stonyhurst.

I have dwelt at some length on the biographical background because these are crucial years in Hopkins's poetical growth, years in which he came to question ever more closely the propriety of practising his art. In general the poems of this period in his life, apart from those written at Oxford, are disappointing in comparison with the achievement of the St. Beuno's period. For one thing Hopkins was for much of the time removed from the kind of natural setting that he needed for refreshment and even when, as at Oxford and Stonyhurst, the setting was congenial he clearly had vocational difficulties that occupied and exhausted him. The centre of his poetry shifts after his ordination and naturally enough a group of his poems bears more immediately upon his vocation: the priest comforting Felix Randal; administering communion to the bugler; pleased at the innocent responsiveness of a boy in his Oxford congregation (*The Handsome Heart*) or as an example of brotherly affection (*The Brothers*). Then there are the two sets of devotional verses *The May Magnificat* and *The Blessed Virgin compared to the Air we Breathe*. *Felix Randal* apart, none of these poems has the finish, complexity and vitality of the earlier period. In general, Hopkins's grip is not secure and one is conscious too often of strain in the writing. However, over the six years before his going to Ireland there are some ten poems in which one feels that his powers are fully engaged and that in achievement almost match the St. Beuno's work.

The first considerable poem written after his ordination was *The Loss of the Eurydice*. It obviously invites comparison with the *Deutschland* and in such a comparison must be regarded as something of a failure. True, it is less obviously meditative, more a ballad in its ordering; some twenty of the stanzas contribute to the narrative with nine at the end making the spiritual application. The restricted stanza form—the first, second and fourth lines carrying four stresses with a third line of three; a rhyme scheme a, a, b, b; sprung rhythm throughout—does not allow the poet sufficient freedom of movement to achieve the fluidity he requires. Occurring as they do in couplets, extravagant rhymes which he carries off superbly in the *Deutschland* and in many of the sonnets, draw attention to itself only too frequently, for example, all un-/fallen; aerial, burial; fully, on, bullion; seamen—be men; he C/ame, electric; portholes, mortals, etc. There is a loss of concentrated energy too in the language, compare 'whirl-wind-swivellèd snow' (*Deutschland*) with

> But his eye no cliff, no coast or
> Mark makes *in the rivelling snowstorm*

Occasionally there is bathos:

> Till a lifebelt and God's will
> Lend him a lift from the sea-swill.

The effect of 'and' here is to give 'a lifebelt' and 'God's will' an even weight in the line, an error in poetic tact inconceivable in the earlier poems. Even a phrase like 'brown-as-dawning-skinned', expressive as it is, is perhaps over-elaborate for this ballad-like narrative context. The sorrowing over the 'unconfessed' in the *Deutschland* is expressed magnificently but in this poem the handling of the equivalent section is at times clumsy:

> He was but one like thousands more,
> Day and night I deplore,
>   My people and born own nation,
> Fast foundering own generation.

The obviousness of the rhyming here and the unreward-ing repetition and placing of 'own' interfere with the weight required for so serious a theme. The feminine rhymes of the last stanza of the poem weaken the rhetorical effect, unsatisfying both to eye and ear.

Not that the poem is to be lightly dismissed. The sudden oncoming of the storm and its progress ('. . . you were a liar, O blue March day.') and the physical violence of the imagery, consonant with the capsizing ship, have their proper force. If the *Eurydice* had preceded the *Deutschland* it would have been seen as a rehearsal for the greater work; as it is it shows a considerable falling off.

Written at Stonyhurst the *May Magnificat* of which Hopkins said that he saw 'little good but the freedom of the rhythm' is metrically close to the *Eurydice*, the only change being the reduction of four stresses in the last line of the stanza to three. The poem is memorable for the freshness of the spring images in the familiar Hopkins vein, the 'strawberry-breasted throstle', the 'drop-of-blood-and-foam-dapple' of the apple orchards and the exquisite lines:

> And azuring-over greybell makes
> Wood banks and brakes wash wet like lakes
> And magic cuckoocall
> Caps, clears, and clinches all—

'Greybell' perfectly applies to the blue-bell in bud, as does the 'azuring-over' to the greybells becoming blue-bells. The fresh, supple stalks of the blue-bells 'wash wet like lakes' because the drifts of them swaying suggest light on moving water.

Hopkins never returned to the stanza forms of the *Eurydice* or the *May Magnificat*. Possibly he found them too restrictive. In both poems there are awkwardnesses, in rhyming and transitions from stanza to stanza frequent enough to suggest that the challenge had not been fully met.

2

Whatever Hopkins's vocational difficulties may have been when he returned to Oxford, there is no doubt of his continuing aesthetic response to it. The profound sadness with which he records the cutting down of poplars at Binsey is a measure of his attachment to the surrounding countryside. His celebration of Oxford as the one-time home of Duns Scotus in *Duns Scotus's Oxford* allows him to praise the city in spite of the 'base and brickish skirt' that now separates the old town from its 'neighbour-nature'.

Binsey Poplars is one of the few free lyrics that Hopkins wrote. It is in sprung rhythm with lines carrying as many as six stresses and as few as two. The flexibility of the verse allows it to respond sensitively to all the demands made on it. The two opening lines present the poplars, remembered as leafy cages defying the 'leaping' sun that is trying to penetrate them, immediately to be followed by the dirge-like 'all felled, felled, are all felled'. Not one of them has been spared—these trees that so subtly once cast their shadows on river and bank. Notice how 'dandled' tenderly suggests a swaying movement and 'sandalled' a light-footedness as though the fleeting shadow movements were walking earth and water.

Having established the inscape of the trees as they were and the appalled sense of their loss Hopkins proceeds in the remainder of the poem to affirm our responsibility towards the natural world. The reverence he has shown in the poetry of the St. Beuno's period is here maintained without, however, invoking overtly Christ or a divine energy. Man's destructiveness is seen for what it is; even when 'we mean / To mend her we end her'. This scene is 'unselved' and will never again be experienced for what it was: '. . . like this slick and seeing ball / But a prick will make no eye at all', an image that carries before all else Hopkins's pain of loss and we recall his earlier experience at Stonyhurst when the ash-tree was cut down ('I wished to die and not to see the inscapes of the world destroyed any more').

The resources of sprung rhythm, internal rhyme (hack: rack; dandled: sandalled; mend her: end her), dissonance (*wind*: *wan*dering; sleek: prick; mean: mend) and alliteration, are all now here with a precise control that achieves a most satisfying unity. It is one of those English lyrics that aspires towards the condition of music.

Duns Scotus's Oxford begins with a delighted evocation of the 'towery', 'branchy between towers' city, with its associated sounds of birds and bells. Even though the direct encounter of old city and countryside has been interrupted, ruined by mean building, the air is still that breathed by Duns Scotus, a city haunted by him 'who of all men most sways my spirits to peace'. Hopkins had begun to study Scotus, the great mediaeval Christian philosopher, as long ago as August 1872:

> At this time I had first begun to get hold of the copy of Scotus on the *Sentences* . . . and was flush with a new stroke of enthusiasm. It may come to nothing or it may be a mercy from God. But just then when I took in any inscape of the sky or sea I thought of Scotus.

When Hopkins says that Scotus is the 'rarest-veinèd

unraveller' of reality and that his spirits are swayed to
peace by him he is clearly saying something of high
importance to himself. Opinions vary as to the precise
nature of Hopkins's indebtedness to him. That Scotus
was a kindred spirit, that the grain of their minds had
much in common is clear, but the basic attitude of Hopkins towards the natural world, with his consciousness of
inscaping and instress, was well-established before he read
Scotus; his theological indebtedness lies outside the
scope of this commentary.

The poem that follows *Duns Scotus's Oxford*, the tribute
to the genius of Purcell, is one of the most difficult poems
to elucidate and were it not for Hopkins's own glosses the
drift of it might well have remained unclear. It is of
interest to find in a letter to Bridges, Hopkins declaring
that 'My sonnet means "Purcell's music is none of your
d—d subjective rot (so to speak)".' and to enquire what
he meant by 'subjective rot'. After expressing his dearest
wish that fortune should have favoured Purcell's spirit in
spite of his dying outside the Catholic Church ('listed to
a heresy, here'), Hopkins declares that what searches him
most deeply in Purcell's music is its 'forged feature . . . the
rehearsal of own, of abrupt self'. If the stamp of 'abrupt
self' is the quality that beyond all others commends the
music to him, in what sense is it not subjective? The developed image of the 'stormfowl' is presumably intended
to make this clear. The behaviour of the bird when
preparing for flight ('meaning motion') with a flurry
of wings is not self-conscious. In spite of itself its true
nature, in all its lovely and complex attributes, is revealed.
So Purcell's music is not self-regarding but displays the
inescapable self-hood of its creator. (The sonnet *As king-
fishers catch fire, dragonflies draw flame* embodies more clearly

Hopkins's conception of self-hood.) It is the glory of Purcell that he 'uttered in notes the very make and species of man as created both in him and in all men generally'.

Of the poems of this period that have not received comment three especially are worth attention: *Peace*, *Spring and Fall*, and *Inversnaid*.

Peace, a curtal sonnet in alexandrines, looks backwards to the dove images in the *Deutschland* and in its underlying tormentedness forward to the terrible sonnets. The whole effect of the sonnet is of moving from restlessness, related to a conception of an insecure and unrewarding peace, to a true peace, born of patience that 'plumes to Peace' as an active not passive state. The underlying insecurity is suggested by the reiteration of 'peace' culminating in the line 'that *piece*meal *peace* is poor *peace*. What pure *peace* allows . . .' Peace here is without a capital, it belongs to an inferior order of experience. But Peace the offspring of Patience is attuned to the divine nature. The thirst for peace is beautifully caught in the circling image of the wooddove, ready to alight but not settling, and in the striking formation 'under be', much stronger than 'be under' for suggesting the hunger for a sustaining peace. The inversion 'to own my heart' for 'to my own heart' is in some sense unfortunate because 'to own' looks so like an infinitive. The risk taken in the interests of what Hopkins must have felt to be rhetorically more satisfying is here, I think, too great. The use of the half-line at the end of the sonnet is another example of Hopkins's metrical resourcefulness. 'He comes to brood and sit,' is assertive and emphatic. The dove as symbol for peace and for the Holy Ghost is a familiar one; it is characteristic of Hopkins that the poem should depend for its success on the precise 'wild wooddove' with its 'shy wings', 'roaming', etc. The physical images are basic and the moral significance is never divorced from them to become a tame, symbolic cliché. The elusiveness of Peace, the intermittent visitation of peace, the being deprived of a Peace that cannot co-exist with the threat and actuality of conflict, teaches the soul God's gift of patience. In the end the poem is about a state of mind, a craving for an ultimate Peace, for a final stillness at the centre, the expectation that patience will lead to a divine visitation. The progress of the poem is, then, from the 'round me roaming' dove, by way of a recognition of how hard Peace is to win, to the image of the nesting bird, fertile in its stillness.

Turn now to *Spring and Fall*, one of the most perfect of Hopkins's poems, a lyric that can hold its own with the choicest of shorter lyrics in English. The poem 'is not founded on any real incident' (Hopkins to Bridges); it is, however, significant that there is a Goldengrove near St. Bueno's. Hopkins imagines a child weeping over the falling leaves (the trees once in leaf are now *un*leaving). He is struck by a freshness of mind that can grieve over the fallen leaves with a degree of concern that in maturity is focused on the common human lot. Alas, this is a temporary phase. In later life Margaret will still weep and know why she is weeping, but it will not be for such causes as the fall of the leaf. Unsuspecting she has been stirred to tears by the source of all sorrows, the fact of man's fallen nature, the common sadness of a mortality to which she is heir. In truth (without knowing it) she is weeping for herself.

According to a letter to Bridges, Hopkins set the poem to plain-chant. The phrasing of the poem as it stands is so exquisite that one doubts whether it could gain in the

E

process. The poem is in sprung rhythm couplets, four stresses to the line. Hopkins gives two stresses to Márgarét in addressing the child. This makes for a deliberateness in speaking the name, possibly with a slight questioning inflection in preparation for the crucial question that is to follow. The vocabulary, as is appropriate to the subject, is of extreme simplicity; the Anglo-Saxon style formations 'unleaving', 'wanwood', 'leafmeal' have an air of simplicity about them that is entirely fitting.

The tenderness that governs the poem as a whole finds its definition in part through the falling cadences that end the first nine lines. The last seven of these lines with their open-vowel endings—'man, you; can you; older: colder; sigh: lie: why;' (notice the triplet)—maintain the mournfulness of tone and theme. They are followed by the strong but muted relationship between 'name' and 'same'. The next two lines are of notable quality:

> Nor mouth had, no nor mind, expressed
> What heart heard of, ghost guessed: . . .

The usual organs for the shaping and uttering of thought, 'mind' and 'mouth', fail to formulate the message that 'heart' and 'ghost' (spirit) intuitively pick up. The contrast between the two lines, the first strong in its negation, denial of normal expectation, the second almost whispered, where the consonantal near-rhymes 'heart: heard' and 'ghost: guessed' suggest in their minor key relationship the secret insight, the still small voice.

Spring and Fall for all its formal strictness achieves an internal freedom that carries conversational ease in the handling of the gravest of themes. It demonstrates possibilities of sprung rhythm not hitherto explored by

Hopkins. Alliteration and stress in combination have normally made for an unusually bold and emphatic verse but in this poem they sustain a refined and consistently withdrawn quality that allows the word 'blight' to take on a terrible power.

Hopkins visited Inversnaid on Loch Lomond for a few hours when he was for a short period performing parish duties in Glasgow; the outcome of this was the short lyric *Inversnaid*. The piece may be described as a nature poem without qualification. Sprung rhythm is used with an almost jaunty effect as it leans forward to carry the sense of the lively, fast-flowing stream. The imagery is direct with a solid definition that comes from a loving intentness on the part of the observer. The energy of the river in spate is caught in 'rollrock' as well as in 'roar'. The *'horseback brown'* image is particularly apt with its suggestion of glossiness and depth of colour. 'Flutes' conveys something like undulating as in a fluted column. 'Twindles', a Hopkins invention, combines twine and wind with the possibility of dwindle, too: that is, the froth is pictured as moving forward erratically at the will of the current or the 'bonnet of froth' may be seen as turning and twisting at the top of the fall with a kind of hesitation before going over, hence 'over the broth' suggests the black pool below. 'Fell-frowning' gives the sense of shadow-casting hillside and the idea of fatality— developed in the whirlpool image 'rounds and rounds Despair to drowning'. 'Degged' =splashed—'degging-can' is still known in the north-west for watering-can, a good example of Hopkins making a dialect word feel at home, carrying its meaning with it. The 'beadbonny' ash —the mountain ash adorned with berries leans out over the stream as a fisherman might sit. The last stanza of the poem again proclaims Hopkins's love of the unspoilt inscapes of the world and ends with a prayer that they should remain undisturbed.

To sum up: in this middle phase Hopkins can be seen moving in a number of directions both in choice of theme and metrical invention. The element of continuity is there in the *May Magnificat, Duns Scotus's Oxford, Henry Purcell*; they carry on the ecstatic vein. *Peace* looks backward, as we have seen, to the *Deutschland* and forward to the terrible sonnets. The exercise of his priestly office produced several devotional poems not of a consistently high quality. Two or three poems based on episodes occurring in the course of his duties, *The Bugler's First Communion, Brothers, Felix Randal* are marked by a somewhat disturbing emotionalism. I sense a degree of hysteria that interferes with my acceptance of them as among the best of Hopkins. A number of the poems centre on human figures and in *Andromeda*, exceptionally, on an allegorical subject. The Scotus sonnet is a fine and moving tribute. In the Purcell sonnet the powerful images of the stormfowl are possibly developed to a point where the symbolic significance is overlaid and external commentary is required for adequate elucidation. Hopkins's individual human subjects are normally idealised, whereas man in the mass—'dear and dogged man'—is seen as the despoiler of nature and sadly out of tune with God and nature. There is consequently a clouding over as the preoccupation with the human obtrudes. The natural world becomes something of a reproachful framework, an Eden-garden in process of ruin. There is a tenderness for the young that finds supreme expression in *Spring and Fall* but the *Bugler* and the *Brothers* have it, too, even though the expression of it is less searching. *The Leaden*

Echo and the Golden Echo completed in 1882 is probably best linked to the fragment of the projected tragedy of *St. Winefred.*

3

Before turning to the 'terrible sonnets', it is convenient here to bring together works relating to St. Winefred's Well. The well in question is at Holywell within walking distance of St. Beuno's. Hopkins made his first visit to it in 1874:

> Barraud and I walked over to Holywell and bathed at the well and returned very joyously. The sight of the water in the well as clear as glass, greenish like beryl or aquamarine, trembling at the surface with the force of the springs, and shaping out the five foils of the well, quite drew and held my eyes to it. . . . The strong unfailing flow of the water and the chain of cures from year to year all these centuries *took hold of my mind* with wonder at the bounty of God in one of His saints, the sensible thing so naturally and gracefully uttering the spiritual reason of its being. . . .' (my italics).

The well did indeed take hold of his mind; he was, as a poet, to return to it time and again almost to the end of his life. In 1877 in a letter, obviously replying to an enquiry of Bridges, he writes:

> Who was St. Beuno? Is he dead? Yes, he did that much 1200 years ago, if I mistake not. He was St. Winefred's uncle and raised her to life when she died in defence of her chastity and at the same time he called out her famous spring, which fills me with devotion every time I see it.

In 1879 in a letter to Bridges, Hopkins declares that he 'has a greater undertaking on hand than any yet, a tragedy on St. Winefred's martyrdom. . . .' The tragedy was never finished but important fragments remain, *The Leaden Echo and the Golden Echo*, and parts of three scenes, the most important of which is the soliloquy of Caradog after he has murdered Winefred. The chorus and the fragments should be read together because of their common theme.

The Leaden Echo and the Golden Echo must be considered, then, as a dramatic chorus. It is based upon questionings and a reply to those questionings: what can be done to arrest the passing of physical beauty, the coming of decay and death? Is there no cure for our mortality? Is despair the necessary condition to which man is reduced? There is a way out, comes the reply, whereby beauty may be saved: give it 'back to God, beauty's self and beauty's giver. / See; not a hair is, not an eyelash lost.' The dedication of beauty to God is its proper end; it can only be retained by returning it to its source. The chorus was finished in 1882 but work on the tragedy of St. Winefred continued on and off until 1886. What, remains of it falls into three scenes: In the first (Act I, scene i) Winefred's father, Teryth, is seen with her. He is instructing her to prepare for the visit of Lord Beuno and his deacon. Winefred goes about her business, her father remains to soliloquize over his love for his daughter and his fears for her safety. The second scene from Act II is set in a wood from which Caradog comes with bloodied sword after murdering Winefred. In a soliloquy of great power he recalls the murder, even doubts whether he has done it, but is self-driven to go over it all again. He refuses to repent. His response is to defend himself 'loyal

to his own soul, laying his own law down'. But he
realizes that in destroying Winefred he has removed the
object of his desires and so has maimed himself:

What do now then?   Do?
Nay,

Deed-bound I am; one deed treads all down here'
    cramps all doing. What do? Not yield,
Not hope, not pray; despair; ' ay, that: brazen despair
    out,
Brave all, and take what comes . . .

He has nothing but contempt for the crowd that now
approaches:

Whose bloods I reck no more of, ' no more rank with
    hers
Than sewers with sacred oils.

Observe that it is Winefred's earthly beauty that Caradog would have ravished and with its destruction he has
nothing to hold on to and must live to brazen out despair.
This is obviously relevant to the leaden echo movement
as is the 'sacred oils' image that he attaches to Winefred,
to the golden echo.

The third fragment of the play spoken by Beuno is
clearly the unfinished ending, for it is placed 'After Winefred's raising from the dead and the breaking out of the
fountain', a fountain that for centuries to come is to be
the resort of pilgrims:

As long as men are mortal' and God merciful,
So long to this sweet spot,' this leafy lean-over,

This Dry Dene, now no longer dry' nor dumb, but
    moist and musical

> With the uproll and the downcarol' of day and night
>   delivering
>
> Water, which keeps thy name,' (for not in rock
>   written,
>
> But in pale water, frail water,' wild rash and
>   reeling water,
> That will not wear a print,' that will not stain a pen,
> Thy venerable record,' virgin, is recorded).

The themes of *The Leaden Echo and the Golden Echo* are exemplified in the lust that would have destroyed the physical beauty of Winefred and in the miracle of her return to life. Apart from the thematic interest of the chorus and the fragments, there is a technical interest in the bold attempt of Hopkins to devise a new kind of dramatic verse. *The Leaden Echo and the Golden Echo* is based on a sprung rhythm foundation, lines of varying length bearing stresses according to the pulse of the meaning. Rhyming is persistent and gives it for all the freedom of movement a pleasing formality. The advantages of sprung rhythm are here fully displayed as the verse now hurries forward, now hesitates according to the over-riding impulse. For the non-choral fragments Hopkins employs lines of six stresses, unrhymed, which combine in flexible verse paragraphs occasionally interrupted by a telling half-line of three stresses. The over-all principle is of three stresses to each half-line. It carries admirably the nervous, distraught soliloquy of Caradog and is used with impressive lyrical effect in Beuno's final speech. Unfortunately its effectiveness in dialogue is not adequately explored; the first fragment when Teryth and Winefred are together has only ten lines of dialogue and these of a stiff, rather clumsy character. It is interesting to note, however, that Hopkins is not prepared to follow the common habit of Victorian poets of writing blank verse tragedies but goes his own way boldly experimenting with a new form of unrhymed verse for dramatic use.

Associated in theme with the St. Winefred's well material is the sonnet, *To what serves Mortal Beauty*, probably the second poem written after his going to Dublin. Hopkins, the poet, was, as we have seen, joyfully responsive to the manifestations of beauty both in the natural world and in man. As priest he had to be scrupulously concerned with beauty's proper end. In *To what serves Mortal Beauty* he gives his most concentrated expression to this preoccupation. In the first line of the poem the word 'dangerous' occurs in a powerful parenthesis, suspended between a dash and a semi-colon. The effect is arresting and, although the poem goes on to exemplify the influence of beauty by referring to 'those lovely lads' (not Angles but angels) whose appearance caught the eye of St. Gregory, the word 'dangerous' hovers over it. The argument of the remainder of the sonnet declares that it is in the nature of man to worship something and that he should love what is most worth loving—'men's selves'. The attributes of the self are revealed in the human form ('self-flashes off frame and face'—cf. 'fire that breaks from thee' in *The Windhover*). How, then, are we to accommodate ourselves to this, heaven's gift? Recognize it for what it is, God's gift, and, accepting it as such, let it alone in favour of 'God's better beauty, grace' lest, the implication appears to be, it becomes an end in itself. The measure of the powerful impact of mortal, physical beauty given in the second and third lines, 'O-seal-that-so feature', etc., indicates a beauty so striking that it cries out for some kind of permanent embodiment. Even Purcell's music has to give way before the challenge of this 'prouder form'.

Questions

1. Compare 'Binsey Poplars' with Wordsworth's poem 'Nutting' or with Cowper's 'The Poplar Field'.

2. 'Take breath and read it with the ears, as I always wish to be read, and my verse becomes all right.' Even if you do find it a help to read the poetry of Hopkins aloud, what kind of difficulties still remain?

3. Discuss Hopkins's success in introducing human beings into his verse (for example Felix Randal, Margaret in *Spring and Fall*, the *Brothers*).

4. '. . . our whole civilisation is dirty, yea filthy, and especially in the north': how far is this attitude reflected in Hopkins's poetry?

5. Hopkins prefaces his sonnet to Henry Purcell with the comment: 'He uttered in notes the very make and species of man as created both in him and in all men generally.' Substituting 'verse' for 'notes' in this comment, apply it to Hopkins's poetry.

6. Write a critical appreciation of those poems of Hopkins which derive from his response to children.

DUBLIN, 1884-1889

Of the twelve years Hopkins lived after his ordination, only four were spent in parish work; nearly one was spent in the third year of his novitiate at Roehampton; the remainder in teaching classics at Stonyhurst and at University College, Dublin. The fact that he was for nearly seven years appointed to teaching posts in his own field of classical studies shows in itself care both for his welfare and the use of his peculiar gifts. His appointment to the Chair of Greek at University College in 1884, sounds grander than it was in fact. 'The house we are in, the College, is a sort of ruin and for purposes of study very nearly naked. And I have more money to buy books than room to put them in.' The post involved a great deal of examination work for Catholic colleges outside University College, and Hopkins found this particularly exacting. There is evidence to show that he had time on his hands at Stonyhurst and at University College except for periods of stress when the examinations were on. The amount of time he gave in his last years to the study of music and to musical composition was much greater than to writing poetry. His desperate unhappiness in Ireland was complex in its origin. His health, never robust, deteriorated; his remoteness from England ('rare-dear Britain'), his family and friends, made him feel cut off; the political tensions in Ireland produced divided loyalties in him; and he suffered from loneliness. Beyond all these factors lay

those spiritual strains that find expression in the series of
poems that have come to be known as the 'terrible sonnets'. It has to be borne in mind, however, that this great
sonnet sequence reflects the poet's deepest concerns and
that day-to-day life is not lived unrelieved. Hopkins could
write *Harry Ploughman* as late as 1887, an epithalamion
(incomplete) even later, and the beautiful unfinished
Ashboughs (1885?) in the vein of the St. Beuno's period.
He enjoyed a holiday in Wales in 1886 which encouraged
him to tinker with his *St. Winefred's Well* tragedy. His
letters over this period reflect poignantly something of
his deep distress but they reflect, too, the busy intellectual life of a poet enjoying mature speculation in a number of fields. He was a priest always conscious of his
vocation, subject to the special strains imposed by it. It
was the calling of his choice and most of his work is, in
its essential qualities, governed by it. Hopkins lived a life
of exceptional intellectual and spiritual vitality, in the
course of which he produced a small body of great
poetry. Any approach should exclude an impure pity. In
the practical details of life he probably suffered from an
excessive scrupulosity; the acceptance of a cup of tea or
the award of half a mark was capable of producing a
minor crisis. There is evidence that he imposed a self-
discipline that exceeded the requirements of his order and
induced scarcely tolerable strains. The conflicts that in-
form so much of his later poetry are on the tragic scale
and his greatness as a poet lies in a boldness of treatment
that securely contains them, and, in achieving this control,
makes language do his bidding with a confidence that is
truly Shakespearean.

2

Spelt from Sibyl's Leaves may be regarded as a prelude to the group of sonnets expressing extreme spiritual torment and aridity. Described by Hopkins as 'the longest sonnet ever written', it employs eight stresses to the line and exploits to the full the resources of sprung rhythm. The poet states that the sonnet is 'made for performance and that its performance is not reading with the eye but loud, leisurely, poetical (not rhetorical) recitation, with long rests, long dwells on the rhyme and other marked syllables. . . . This sonnet should be almost sung. . . .'

A common error of interpretation in discussing this sonnet is, I believe, to take 'hornlight' in the third line as having to do with the setting moon. W. H. Gardner, for example, invokes Milton's 'hornèd moon' to support such a reading. It is, however, characteristic of Hopkins to avoid literary echoes of this kind: his apprehension of the natural world is always marked by its directness. Such literary associations as 'hornèd moon' interfere with that directness. If 'hornlight' has an obvious meaning it is surely that of light shining through horn or of light possessing the colour quality of horn. Father Raymond Scholes has made this point convincingly in his gloss on 'hornlight' (*Immortal Diamond*, p. 208). Once this reading is accepted the reader is preserved from further errors of interpretation that arise from finding primarily musical implications in the relationships between 'hornlight', 'wound', 'strains', and 'attunable'.

Father W. A. M. Peters, having taken hornlight to refer to the light of the setting moon, can write (*Gerard Manley Hopkins*, 1948, p. 164):

But there is music in these lines. Is it because we not only see the moon setting but hear her go down on the notes of the 'horn'? How well the choice of 'strains' fits here! And this wonderful strain of music explains the use of 'attunable' as well.

The consequences of forcing 'strains' and 'wound' into a system of musical associations is to enfeeble them. They are both powerful verbs, not mildly active, but carrying the full weight of evening pressing on, striving to become night. 'Attunable' does not call for special explanation. Evening is 'attunable' because it makes for harmony, tending to give to all things a common, subdued quality of appearance.

Instead of going to the literary *horned moon* the reader would be better advised to consider the function of *horn* in *lanthorn* and *hornbook*. The lanthorn gives the soft, parchment glow that is required and hornbook suggests a spelling out of the mystery written in the sky—alpha and omega, the first and the last.

That Hopkins is concerned with a pervasive light in the sky, even, clear, mellow, is supported by the neighbouring 'hoarlight' and the later 'bleak light'. As the eye moves from the west to the zenith it is conscious of these gradations, of daylight draining away and the darkness inexorably closing in. The sonnet relies for its effect on the evocative power of images of slow, relentless transition. Evening 'strains' to be night, the 'womb-of-all, home-of-all'. With the dying day, shapes, contours, identities lose their clarity. Here is a parable for all to read, telling of the predicament of the human soul in which light and darkness are contending. Hence the importance of giving to 'wound' the strong, relentless pressure that the later 'spool' image will maintain, an image which in its turn will lead into that of the 'rack'. Thus 'wound' is the clue to the poem's direction. If the reader wishes to preserve a musical relationship between 'wound' and 'hornlight', it should remain as a poignant, marginal echo reinforcing, not distracting from, the primary meaning of 'wound'.

No poem of Hopkins is more rewarding for the pains of close study and repeated reading aloud than *Spelt from Sibyl's Leaves*. It has, in its universal application, the force of a great parable: the oracle is ours and the tale told is for us. In this poem Hopkins's personal suffering is kept in the background, whereas in the 'terrible sonnets' the 'I' is central.

These sombre sonnets of conflict and desolation, to which we now turn, have their prose counterpart in Hopkins's correspondence with Bridges. In April, 1885, he speaks of 'that coffin of weakness and dejection in which I live'; in May he can write, on sending two sonnets to Bridges: 'if ever anything was written in blood one of these was'. (The poem in question according to Bridges was *Carrion Comfort*, but the description would apply as aptly to *No worst, there is none* or *I wake and feel the fell of dark*.) In September of the same year he complains: 'it kills me to be time's eunuch and never to beget'. (*Thou art indeed just, Lord* and *The fine delight that fathers thought* are the most poignant expressions of this sense of sterility.) It is ironical that in his exhaustion he should find the inspiration for at least six sonnets which in their artistry show Hopkins at the height of his powers.

The image with which *Spelt from Sibyl's Leaves* ends, of the rack where man is 'self-wrung, self-strung, sheathe-and shelterless', prepares the way for further expressions of inner conflict, more painful because intensely personal. In *Carrion Comfort* the rack image is in a measure carried over; the victim refuses to give way even though 'the last few strands of man' are weakened; the will to defy despair has at all costs to hold. Despair is seen to be the enemy: the victim, tested to breaking point, questions the aggressor:

> But ah, but O thou terrible, why wouldst thou rude on me
> Thy wring-world right foot rock? lay a lionlimb against me? scan
> With darksome devouring eyes my bruisèd bones? and fan,
> O in turns of tempest, me heaped there; me frantic to avoid thee and flee?

Passive, terrified, 'heaped there', desperate to escape, the victim answers the question: it is a necessary ordeal imposed to separate the wheat from the chaff; it is sent from God and the aggressor is God. The transition from 'O thou terrible' to 'The hero whose heaven-handling flung me, foot trod me', by way of the winnowing wind imagery, from deepest dejection to apparent triumph, leads us to the anguished self-questioning of 'cheer whom though?': was it self-congratulation after all? If so, the defeat is a desperate one, the conflict unresolved.

The 'wrestling' of *Carrion Comfort*, with its wild-beast imagery of 'lion-limb', 'darksome devouring eyes', 'bruisèd bones', carries the quality of nightmare with it. In the next sonnet, *No worst, there is none*, the apparently never-ending torment finds definition in equally nightmarish terms: the victim this time hangs on the cliff-face with a sheer drop, 'no-man-fathomed', beneath him. Suffering breeds more suffering; the anguished cries, like the moans of driven cattle, contribute to a symphony of pain, take their place in the 'chief-woe, world-sorrow' ('the blight man was born for'). The only relief is in the sleep that follows exhaustion but this, by implication, is only a temporary, precarious retreat, a mere refuge from the whirlwind. The terms in which this magnificent sonnet is expressed would appear to derive from King Lear. How far Hopkins was conscious of this is impossible to say: his dislike of borrowings and the sheer force of the poem would seem to exclude deliberate adoption. *No worst there is none*, is probably one of the sonnets to which Hopkins refers in a letter to Bridges: 'they came like inspirations unbidden and against my will'.

Spelt from Sibyl's Leaves, Carrion Comfort and, to some extent, *No worse, there is none*, are night-pieces: theirs is a darkness in which the sufferer is racked, is exposed on the anvil to the hammer, wrestles with God; it is a darkness in which time has no meaning ('that night, that year of now done darkness'), where there is no end to the wretchedness, only exhaustion. In a fourth sonnet in the series, *I wake and feel the fell of dark*, darkness becomes palpable; darkness is figured as a smothering animal pelt. 'Fell' is doubtless the archaic noun, as in 'flesh and fell', with overtones of the adjectival sense, 'cruel'. The image is essentially claustrophobic: there appears to be no escape; the black hours have seemed endless but the prospect is of years, a lifetime of suffering. Cries for help are apparently unheard, 'like dead letters sent / To dearest him that lives alas! away'. (Cf. 'Mary, mother of us, where is your relief?') Thus cut off from the sources of consolation the 'wretch' is thrown in upon himself and

F*

by God's decree is filled with a bitter revulsion at what he finds there: 'self yeast of spirit a dull dough sours'. Only the 'sweating selves' of the damned can be in a more desperate plight.

The poet's isolation is also the theme of *To seem the stranger lies my lot*, the sonnet that precedes *I wake and feel the fell of dark*. This sonnet is different in manner from its neighbours. The language is austere and the poignancy depends largely on the forthright definition of a three-fold separation: a separation that is physical, from family and country; a spiritual separation, by virtue of beliefs not shared; and a political apartness, in that the poet is torn between sympathy with the Irish and love of his own country, 'wife to my creative thought'. Even so he can still give and receive love, but what is above all else responsible for his sense of estrangement is the interdiction, whether from heaven or hell, that stops or ignores what for him is most precious to express. The curious use of 'began' as a noun is, I think, related to the sonnet's central theme, the sense of being cut off from fertilising and refreshing relationships with either God or man: a 'beginning' implies an end, a 'began' suggests an arrested beginning, of his having gone so far and then been halted, unfulfilled, when the desire is for completion.

The five sonnets that have been discussed are full of painful conflict fought in isolation, exhausting and unremitting. The two sonnets that follow, *Patience, hard thing!* and *My own heart let me more have pity on*, offer at least the possibility of relief. In *Patience, hard thing!* patience, like the ivy, is seen to be parasitic; it cannot exist without suffering and defeat to feed on:

> . . . Natural heart's ivy, Patience masks
> Our ruins of wrecked past purpose. There she basks
> Purple eyes and seas of liquid leaves all day.

The 'purple eyes' (ivy berries) suggest both watching the sufferer and feeding on his sufferings, a very unpleasant image. (It is relevant here to recall 'the darksome devouring eyes' of *Carrion Comfort*). Until the last three lines of the sonnet the language is close to that of the sonnets of deprivation:

> We hear our hearts grate on themselves: it kills
> To bruise them dearer. Yet the rebellious wills
> Of us we do bid God bend to him even so.

Patience, as an active principle in the last three lines is shown at work filling the honeycombs. The question 'where is he who more and more distils delicious kindness?' is not answered directly. It may well be a reference to Christ as the model of patience.

In *My own heart let me more have pity on* the poet realizes that he has driven himself too hard and has not shown sufficient charity towards himself. He must break out of the circle of self-torment in which he is groping fruitlessly and leave comfort room to grow; let joy grow in God's good time. God smiles in benediction when it pleases him—he is not to be forced by over-urgent pleading. The smile comes when least expected even as bright sky appearing between the mountains might light up in front of us 'a lovely mile'.

Of the seven poems that Hopkins was to complete after 1885, four have to do with his spiritual life; the first of these, *That Nature is a Heraclitean Fire*, brings back into his poetry a confidence and sense of illumination

that recalls *The Wreck of the Deutschland*. After an ex-
hilarating opening in which the wind tosses the racing
clouds, drying the mud of yesterday's rain to 'squeezed
dough, crust, dust', evidence of a clean, bright energy at
once creative and destructive, comes the magnificent
affirmation 'Million-fuelèd, nature's bonfire burns on'.
Fire according to Heraclitus is the moving principle
behind the flux of all existence. Hopkins, the poet of
energy, appears at first to be enthralled by it and then
appalled. That man in his special place in the order of
things should be consumed with all else, be so vulnerable,
'beaten level', his 'firedint' extinguished, drowned 'in
enormous dark', is matter for 'pity and indignation'. Then
cutting across the vision of man's extinction comes the
clarion call from the heart declaring the Resurrection:

> Across my foundering deck shone
> A beacon, an eternal beam.' Flesh fade, and mortal trash
> Fall to the residuary worm;' world's wildfire, leave but
>   ash:

At this point a comment on the form of this sonnet
(with three codas) may be of use. The first fourteen lines
give us nature's bonfire creating and extinguishing. There
follows a half-line introducing the first of the codas in
which the appalled sense of man's physical blotting-out
is checked by the heart's knowledge of the Resurrection.
Another half-line 'Across my foundering deck shone'
leads into the second coda telling us that 'mortal trash'
may be safely, indeed contemptuously, reduced to ashes
in the knowledge of the beacon, the eternal beam sig-
nalling 'in a flash, at a trumpet crash' (another half-line),
the identification of man with Christ. This forms the

substance of the third coda in which Hopkins's rhetoric achieves one of its most amazing effects:

I am all at once what Christ is, since he was what I am, and
This Jack, joke, poor potsherd,¹ patch, matchwood, immortal diamond,
                              Is immortal diamond.

The normal confines of the sonnet have to be expanded further than in any earlier poem to encompass the theme. The dramatic transformation in the middle of the fifteenth line is a clear break and makes for a proper balance between the two parts of the poem, so that, although the structure has swollen to twice the conventional length, the logic of the sonnet is confidently preserved. Observe how Jack refers back to Jackself in *My own heart let me more have pity on.* The use of the half-line to introduce each coda and then to complete the poem with the proud affirmation 'Is immortal diamond', had already been tried out with a somewhat similar effect in *Tom's Garland*, and, at an earlier stage, a hint of this ingenious variation for achieving special emphasis is to be seen in the two-word last line, 'Praise him', of the curtal sonnet *Pied Beauty*.

There is not room here for more than a cursory glance at the sonnet in honour of St. Alphonsus Rodriguez. Hopkins wrote it to order, in celebration of the first feast after the canonization of this saint. In so far as St. Alphonsus had lived the humble life of hall-porter for forty, apparently uneventful, years, and is to be compared with those heroes whose exploits are publicly displayed, Hopkins is able in speaking of the saint to reveal something of his own suffering:

> But be the war within, the brand we wield
> Unseen, the heroic breast not outward-steeled,
> Earth hears no hurtle then from fiercest fray.

And, no doubt, the thought so tenderly expressed that God, 'who, with trickling increment, / Veins violets', etc., could give recognition to what was hidden from the human eye, is expressive of a degree of reassurance in Hopkins's own experience.

The ecstatic ring with which the Heraclitean Fire sonnet ends and the feeling of stability that *St. Alphonsus Rodriguez* communicates, might suggest that Hopkins had fought his way through to firm ground again. But the poems that were to follow, *Though art indeed just, Lord*, and *The shepherd's brow, fronting forked lightning*, in a degree contradict this impression.

Thou art indeed just, Lord, in common rhythm like the preceding sonnet, is notable for its simplicity of manner and its dignity. The poet is here speaking out plainly; while acknowledging God's justice he asserts the justice of his own case. The case is put with due deference— 'sir . . . sir'—but the argument appears to be so overwhelming that, were it not God in question, the failure to show some recognition for a lifetime's service would appear outrageous. By introducing images of free-flowing life with the rhetorical pointers, 'See!', 'look' (cf. *Spring* 'all this juice and all this joy') Hopkins defines with terrible poignancy his own sterility; for all his effort he cannot 'breed one work that wakes' and the poem ends with the desperate prayer in which God, the source of all life, is asked to make him fruitful:

> Mine, O thou lord of life, send my roots rain.

By using a verse from *Jeremiah* for the epigraph and first three lines of the sonnet Hopkins is able to open his disputation with God in Jeremiah's terms and to sustain the challenge in the vein of the ancient questionings.

Following hard upon *Thou art indeed just, Lord,* a little over a fortnight later in 1889, came the sonnet *The shepherd's brow, fronting forked lightning,* which has only recently found its rightful place among the completed poems. Bridges had relegated it to the fragments, believing it 'to have been thrown off one day in a cynical mood'. One can see that Bridges was justifiably uneasy about placing it where by date it properly belonged. It is disconcerting to find it so near to *That Nature is a Heraclitean Fire* and *Thou art indeed just, Lord,* because it requires so different a response from the reader. In this sonnet man is seen as through the wrong end of a telescope: how trivial his affairs appear to be when measured by the fall of the angels, 'a story / Of just, majestical, and giant groans'. The frailty of man ('scaffold of score brittle bones'), his humiliating servitude to the body ('Hand to mouth he lives, and voids with shame'), whose every breath is a reminder of death: what does all this add up to? Whatever fancy names we give him, 'Man Jack the man is, just'; and if 'just' means 'that and nothing else', and if Jack means what it did in the Heraclitean Fire sonnet, 'joke, poor potsherd', the poem may be seen as expressing a mood of self-disgust and extreme bitterness. The spectacle of life with its clumsy distortions, as though reflected in metal spoons, enables the poet to take the measure of his own little drama and to see his conflicts and his fussy self-concern reduced to near-insignificance. At the same time the shepherd in fronting the forked lightning is aware of 'The horror and the havoc and the glory / Of it.' The effect of placing man's tiny struggles in perspective against a background of falling angels (reminding him that he cannot compete) is not to deprive him of a sense of glory but to mock his own pretensions. May not Hopkins have come to suspect that there was something over-intense in his former self-appraisals? Where in *Carrion Comfort* the self-questioning had been feverish, is he not now casting a cold eye on man's tendency to strike postures that though expressive of humility are really self-regarding?

Two sonnets, both written in 1887, stand apart from the poetry of spiritual crisis. They are partner pieces in contrast: the one, *Tom's Garland: upon the Unemployed*, of the town; the other, *Harry Ploughman*, of the country. There is not scope here for a detailed discussion of either poem. Hopkins's explanation of *Tom's Garland* (to be found in the notes of all complete editions of the poetry) is a necessary guide to the theme, but even with this guide the argument is not easy to follow. Tom with his garland of hobnails is the foot of society; he is content with his lot of hard work, enough to eat, a good night's sleep. He is free of the anxieties of the rich and the powerful. But what of those who are outside the pale of the social order, the unemployed? They have care in common only, and either fall into despair (become 'Hangdog'), or grow enraged, wolfish: 'their packs infest the age'. I find nothing more difficult to account for than these lines with their animal classifications. There is no suggestion that Tom Heart-at-ease might at any moment be sent to join the packs of 'Loafers, Tramps, Cornerboys, Roughs, Socialists and other pests of society' (Hopkins's note). The animal names that Hopkins applies to the unfortunate seem strangely out of character, especially when one remembers his eloquent 'in a manner I am a communist' letter to Bridges (August 2, 1871), magnanimous and far-sighted. The sonnet has a forced vitality, an unnecessary complexity, and a rhetorical awkwardness which makes reading aloud impossible. How is the reading voice to sustain a connection between 'lustily he his low lot' and 'swings through' when hampered by a three-line paren-thesis? What is interesting is that the intimate sonnets expressive of personal experience move towards a less contorted style in which complexity of expression arises naturally from what is asking to be said, while in the two sonnets under discussion one senses an over-preoccupa-tion with technique, a certain forcing of the verse and a consequent occasional falsity of tone, particularly in *Tom's Garland*.

Harry Ploughman is a more successful poem than *Tom's Garland*; Hopkins is always at ease in the natural world, and here we have a figure in the centre of a landscape. The octave presents the ploughman as through a sculp-tor's eye, the tensed muscles 'featuring in flesh' what they are intent on doing. The sestet, full of movement, catches superbly the strenuous, dedicated action, the wallowing of the plough and the dark soil turning. The use of 'broth' is something of a puzzle. It is as though Hopkins had wanted to balance 'hard' and 'hurdle' by 'broth' and 'breath', and in so doing had given to 'broth' regardless of its meaning the lightness of sound that suited 'flue' (fluff). Another detail of some interest is the compound 'wind-lilylocks-laced' (cf. 'brim, in a flash, full', *Wreck of the Deutschland*). My complaint here is not a grammatical one, but one of propriety: what is sug-gested by 'lilylocks?' Does it combine happily with the masculine qualities of the ploughman? Has the poet been enticed into introducing 'lilylocks-laced' because he liked the alliterative sequence for its movement rather than for any precise quality of colour or texture?

We now come to the last of Hopkins's sonnets, that addressed to the poet Robert Bridges. The two poets had been friends since their Oxford days and their correspondence is a particularly rich one on Hopkins's side; Bridges's letters were probably destroyed when they were returned to him after Hopkins's death. That Hopkins should address this superb sonnet to his friend only a few weeks before he died provides a fitting close to a distinguished friendship. Its rightness of tone and delicacy of control make it both a poignant farewell to poetry and one of the finest compliments ever paid by one poet to another.

It is appropriate, too, that the sonnet has to do with the creative process itself. The masculine poetic insight 'live and lancing like the blowpipe flame' declares itself in penetrating the mind waiting to welcome it. Once fertilised it is the mind's province to cherish the insight, to bring it to fruition. Hence the stress on the process of gestation; the seed lies nourished and developing for nine months, maybe nine years, before the mind becomes the 'mother of immortal song'. Although widowed, no longer visited by the fertilizing flame, the mind is now itself fertile, 'with aim / Now known and hand at work now never wrong.' How true this is of this poem! The sureness of touch that marks the whole sonnet is particularly to be felt in the sestet. For while the sestet returns to the sterility theme and at the same time manages to image the lost power, 'the roll, the rise, the carol, the creation', it is also capable of ending on a note of friendly courtesy, poignantly apologetic:

My winter world, that scarcely breathes that bliss
Now, yields you, with some sighs, our explanation.

When we remember that Hopkins said that certain poems came to him unbidden and against his will he is touching on what is perhaps his tragic flaw:

His poetic genius (wrote Father Devlin) was his very essence, his 'inscape', his special likeness to the Divine Essence. Yet Hopkins the Jesuit behaved to Hopkins the poet as a Victorian husband might to a wife of whom he had come to be ashamed. His muse was a highborn lady, a chaste matron, dedicated to God; but he treated her in public as a slut, and her children as an unwanted and vaguely sinful burden.[1]

There is some satisfaction in finding that he had at the end of his life a proper reverence for his muse. Even the memory of the fine delight that fathers thought was sufficient to inspire one of the saddest and most accomplished sonnets in English.

Questions

1. 'To the greater glory of God': show the relevance of this phrase even to the darkest of Hopkins's sonnets.

2. 'The poetry of Hopkins is probably nearer to that of Herbert than to that of any other English poet.' After reading several of Herbert's poems, e.g., *The Collar*, comment on the validity of this statement.

3. Trace the development of Hopkins's use of the sonnet through its various phases.

[1] *The Sermons and Devotional Writings of Gerard Manley Hopkins*, ed. Christopher Devlin, S.J. (London, 1959).

4. Compare any one of Hopkins's later sonnets with Donne's *Batter my heart, three person'd God*.

5. Select and discuss the poems which you think best show the relationship between Hopkins's response to nature and his deepest religious experience.

FURTHER READING

There is as yet no satisfactory life of Hopkins. The *Life of Hopkins* by F. G. Lahey (1930) is interesting but sketchy. The full-length study by W. H. Gardner, *Gerard Manley Hopkins: A Study of Poetic Idiosyncrasy in Relation to Poetic Tradition,* may be used profitably for reference.

One of the earliest critical assessments appeared in 1932 in F. R. Leavis's *New Bearings in English Poetry;* it is still well worth reading. The recent book on Hopkins by Norman H. Mackenzie, Oliver and Boyd Ltd., 1968, is particularly useful on sprung rhythm and 'enrichment from dialect'. For acute insight into Hopkins's temperament, Christopher Devlin's edition of the *Sermons and Devotional Writings of Gerard Manley Hopkins,* Oxford University Press, 1959, is very valuable, particularly Father Devlin's introductions to the various sections.

NOTES ON ENGLISH LITERATURE

Chief Adviser: JOHN D. JUMP, *Professor of English Literature in the University of Manchester*

General Editor: W. H. MASON, *Lately Senior English Master, The Manchester Grammar School*

12 Dryden **Absalom and Achitophel**
W. GRAHAM, *Sometime Senior English Master, Dame Allan's Boys' School, Newcastle-upon-Tyne*

13 Sheridan **The Rivals, The School for Scandal, The Critic**
B. A. PHYTHIAN, *Senior English Master, The Manchester Grammar School*

14 Shakespeare **King Lear**
HELEN MORRIS, *Principal Lecturer in English, Homerton College, Cambridge*

15 Forster **A Passage to India**
W. H. MASON

16 Chaucer **The Nun's Priest's Tale and The Pardoner's Tale**
R. W. V. ELLIOTT

17 Milton **Paradise Lost, Books IV and IX**
W. GRAHAM

18 Shakespeare **King Richard II**
HELEN MORRIS

19 Browning **Men and Women**
MARK ROBERTS, *Professor of English Literature, University of Belfast*

20 Webster **The White Devil, The Duchess of Malfi**
JOHN D. JUMP, *Professor of English Literature, University of Manchester*

21 George Eliot **Middlemarch**
A. O. J. COCKSHUT, *Fellow of Hertford College, Oxford*

22 Shakespeare **The Winter's Tale**
G. FOX, *Assistant Master, The Manchester Grammar School*

23 Lawrence **Sons and Lovers**
CHRISTOPHER HANSON, *Lecturer in English Literature, University of Manchester*

24 Mrs. Gaskell　　**Sylvia's Lovers**
GRAHAM HANDLEY, *Senior Lecturer in English, All Saints'
College, Tottenham*

25 Shakespeare　　**Antony and Cleopatra**
HELEN MORRIS

26 Wordsworth　　**The Prelude I & II**
W. GRAHAM

27 Forster　　**Howards End**
G. P. WAKEFIELD, *Senior English Master, King George V
School, Southport*

28 Austen　　**Persuasion**
J. R. COATES, *Senior English Master, Hymer's College,
Kingston-upon-Hull*

29 Woolf　　**To the Lighthouse**
W. A. DAVENPORT, *Lecturer in English, Royal Holloway
College*

30 Shaw　　**Man and Superman**
A. W. ENGLAND, *Senior Lecturer in English, Eaton Hall
College of Education, Retford, Notts.*

31 Synge　　**Playboy of the Western World,
Riders to the Sea**
A. PRICE, *Senior Lecturer in Education, Queen's University,
Belfast*

32 Byron　　**Childe Harold III and IV, Vision of
Judgement**
PATRICIA BALL, *Lecturer in English, Royal Holloway College*

33 Shakespeare　　**Othello**
G. P. WAKEFIELD

34 Dickens　　**Bleak House**
PETER DANIEL, *Assistant Master, Ratcliffe College, Leicester*

35 Dickens　　**Hard Times**
GRAHAM HANDLEY

36 Miller **Death of a Salesman**
C. J. PARTRIDGE, *Assistant Professor, Department of English Literature and Language, University of Victoria, B.C., Canada*

37 Shakespeare **Hamlet**
KEITH SAGAR, *Staff Tutor, Extra Mural Dept, University of Manchester*

38 Hopkins **The Poetry of Gerard Manley Hopkins**
H. C. SHERWOOD, *Senior Staff Tutor, Extra Mural Dept, Manchester University*